BANKABLE BUSINESS PLANS
SECOND EDITION

EDWARD G. ROGOFF

FOREWORD BY
JEFF BEZOS
FOUNDER & CEO, AMAZON.COM

ROWHOUSE
PUBLISHING

ROWHOUSE
PUBLISHING

Copyright ©2007 by Edward G. Rogoff

For more information, contact Rowhouse Publishing, 1375 Broadway, Suite 600, New York, NY 10018-7060, (877) 363-9866. Find us on the Internet at www.bankablebusinessplans.com.

Brief excerpts, as submitted from *Annual Statement Studies* by The Risk Management Association ©2006, reprinted with permission of The Risk Management Association.

Library of Congress Cataloging in Publication Data:

    Rogoff, Edward G., 1951-
      Bankable business plans / Edward G. Rogoff; foreword
    by Jeff Bezos. — 2nd ed.
      p. cm.
      Includes bibliographical references and index.
      LCCN 2007921044
      ISBN-13: 978-0-9791522-0-7
      ISBN-10: 0-9791522-0-8

      1. Business planning. 2. New business enterprises—
    Finance. 3. Business enterprises—Finance. I. Title.

HD30.28.R644 2007   658.4'012
                            QBI07-600083
           Printed in Canada

Book and Cover design by Jack Mayer

In memory of my father...
who made the best plans.

CONTENTS

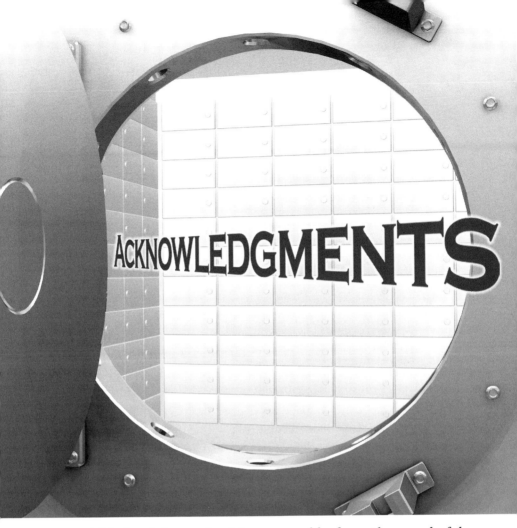

ACKNOWLEDGMENTS

This book has gained immeasurably from the wonderful colleagues with whom I am fortunate to work. Throughout the process, from conceptualization to completion, Mike Shatzkin, my friend and agent, has been essential. Mike possesses one of the most active and creative minds I have ever encountered; you would not be holding this book without his unflagging support and enthusiasm.

I work with an extraordinary group of scholars at Baruch College's Zicklin School of Business at The City University of New York. They include Professors Myung-Soo Lee, Barry Rosen, Marilyn Neimark, Robert Foskey, and Carl Ullman, who shared their extensive knowledge about entrepreneurship and contributed their patient and constructive readings of earlier drafts.

Professor Ramona K. Z. Heck at Baruch College has been a pioneer of thought and research in the realm of family business, which permeates virtually every aspect of entrepreneurship and business creation. I have greatly benefited from her work, from being her colleague, and, most of all, from being her friend. Action Step 8, which deals with potential sources of funding, has been greatly improved by her suggestions.

Professor George Haynes of Montana State University, a leading expert on small-business finance, generously provided guidance on identifying the most common sources of financing for small and startup businesses.

Dr. Pat Imbimbo, Director of the Baruch Career Development Center, imparted her expertise about presenting one's qualifications, and Frank Guarino, a business counselor at the Lawrence N. Field Center for Entrepreneurship at Baruch College, contributed his knowledge of SBA loans, a subject in which he is an unrivaled expert. Yael and Avi Levi, graduate students with significant business experience, masterfully helped shape the financial presentations. Another wonderful graduate student, Enoch Anand, provided expert help with time lines. Carla Hojaiban, a former graduate student of mine, was an especially insightful reader of previous drafts. There was no more knowledgeable reader of earlier drafts than Milt Kamen, a successful entrepreneur and man of great wisdom. He made significant contributions to the concepts and specifics of this book.

My friend and colleague, Professor Alvin N. Puryear, deserves special mention. Not only did he provide indispensable comments on various drafts, but he has also been the guiding force in establishing the teaching of entrepreneurship as a vital course of study at Baruch. As the founding Academic Director of the Field Center, Professor Puryear has provided fundamental insights as to how entrepreneurship should be taught, and how a public college can encourage aspiring entrepreneurs. His commitment to these goals has created a superior educational program for Baruch students and faculty, as well as for Field Center clients. The opportunity to work with Professor Puryear, Baruch students, and Field Center clients has been crucial to my writing this book.

As you will see from reading Bankable Business Plans, I believe that libraries are indispensable in completing the research to support a strong plan. I greatly benefited from the expertise of Baruch College librarian Rita Ormsby, who helped identify the superb resources listed throughout this book.

An extraordinary attorney and wonderful friend, Richard Rosenstein, provided expert guidance on legal issues and embodies the quality of lawyer that successful entrepreneurs need.

I have greatly benefited from being married to a wonderful writer and editor, Perry-Lynn Moffitt, who is now, unexpectedly, an expert on writing business plans. Her thoughtful, patient, and cheerful multiple readings of this book have increased its clarity and eloquence many fold.

Edward G. Rogoff
New York, NY
March 2007

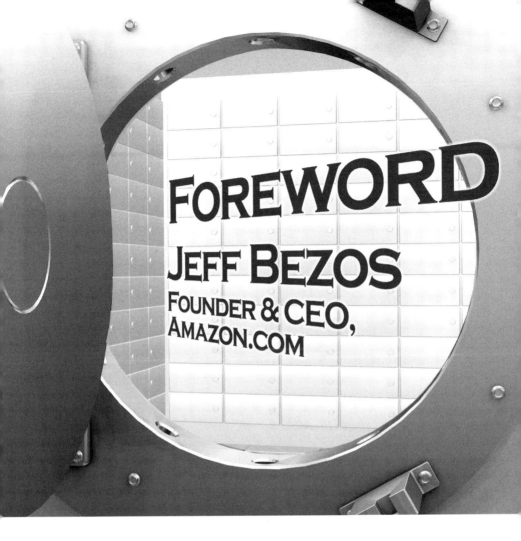

FOREWORD
JEFF BEZOS
FOUNDER & CEO, AMAZON.COM

The wake-up call for Amazon.com came in 1994 when I read that World Wide Web usage was growing at an astonishing 2,300% a year. The Web was a small place then, but something growing that fast can be invisible today and everywhere tomorrow.

I chose books as the first-best product to sell online. At any given time, there are millions of books active and in print around the world. The largest physical superstores can carry only about 100,000 different titles and mall bookstores typically less than 30,000. Amazon.com would be able to offer the complete selection—millions of books—not just what would fit on the physical shelves. That basic idea—complete selection—was the primary way that Amazon.com was going to add genuine, important value for customers in its early days.

A little after that wake-up call, my wife and I left New York City and headed to Seattle. In the car, I wrote the first draft of what would become the Amazon.com business plan. I continued to work on it for weeks after we arrived in Seattle—ultimately locking myself in a research cubicle at a local library with peanut butter sandwiches for days on end so that I wouldn't be distracted. The more I worked on it, the better the plan became.

The process of writing down my thoughts improved my thinking, and helped me practice mentally and visualize what we were going to do. To be sure, my primary motivation for writing the business plan was to help communicate the idea of Amazon.com to prospective investors, but, in hindsight, an incredibly important benefit that came from writing the plan was crisper, more innovative, more customer-focused thinking. After months of effort and presenting the Amazon.com business plan to some 60 different prospective investors, I was lucky enough to find about 20 "angel" investors who put in approximately $50,000 each. Raising $1 million dollars is supposed to be hard, and it was. I doubt it would have been possible at all without an organized business plan.

In July, 1995, we opened for business with an office and a 400-square-foot warehouse in the Color-Tile building in an industrial area south of downtown Seattle. Our expectations for early sales were modest, and the business plan called for a long startup period where customers would slowly learn about and adopt this new way of shopping. But we were surprised immediately. To everyone's astonishment, in the first 30 days, with no advertising, we took orders from customers in all 50 states and 45 countries.

At this point, our growth was so much stronger than expected, that most of the details in the business plan were no longer valid. It's probably the rare business plan that survives the first day of the business being open. Nevertheless, the process of writing the plan forces you to think through many different cases. As a result, when something changes, you're better prepared for it.

So while the business plan had called for us to be small, we quickly scaled up as customers around the world discovered Amazon.com and kept coming back. After nine months, we relocated to a 12,000 square foot fulfillment center, and seven months later we occupied a 45,000 square foot facility.

Building on the initial business plan, Amazon.com was able to raise $8 million in venture capital by 1996 and the following year, we went public. Customers kept asking us to sell additional categories of products (they still do this). So we introduced music CDs, DVDs, and videos in 1998. That same year we opened amazon.co.uk and amazon.de in Europe. The following year we added electronics, tools, toys, and software, and we began allowing other people to sell their merchandise at Amazon.com. In 2000, Amazon.com had more than 3 million square feet of fulfillment center space in the United States. And we had also opened sites for France and Japan.

As we gained experience, our business continued to be built on offering customers selection and convenience. In July of 2001, we added a third pillar to our business plan: low prices. We would be the kind of retailer that works relentlessly to lower prices for customers. With growing volume and increasing operational efficiencies, we've been able to share the savings with customers in the form of lower prices—and we're going to keep doing that.

Even though all the details have changed over the years, many of the original concepts outlined in the first business plan remain central to our business. In addition, even though you can't plan on it, we've also been lucky. We're especially grateful to our customers, and if you bought this book (or anything else) from Amazon.com, thank you.

I knew Ed before I started Amazon.com, and I believe his experiences with his own successful ventures and as a professor of entrepreneurship make him an excellent person to guide you from initial idea through the creation of an effective plan that will serve the needs of your customers and investors.

A strong business plan will not only help you locate the early funds you need, but will also clarify your thinking and serve as a starting blueprint for future growth in what is always a changing world.

All the best, and good luck serving customers!

Jeff Bezos
Seattle, Washington
October 2002

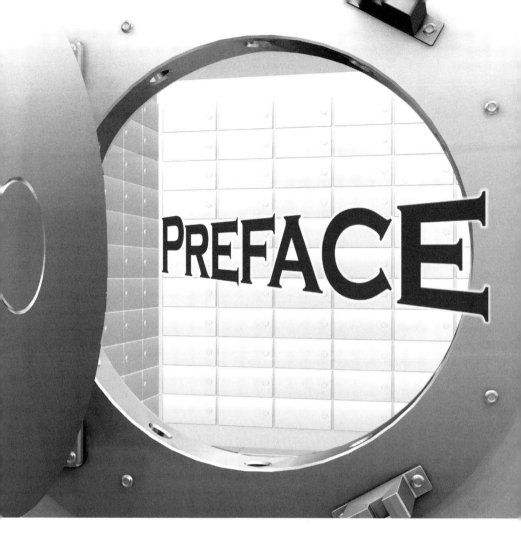

A *bankable business plan* is one that attracts the approval and financing for your venture by addressing the needs of bankers and investors while still accomplishing your own entrepreneurial goals. This book is written with one central purpose: to guide you through the process of creating a bankable business plan, so you can obtain the resources you need to start, build, or buy a business.

My extensive experience in writing my own successful business plans, helping other entrepreneurs create effective plans, and advising funding sources on how to evaluate submitted plans, has taught me that a strong plan is built on a single basic element: it must meet the needs of financial supporters, whether they be bankers, investors, family members, or partners.

I have personally raised more than $100 million from angels, banks, and venture capitalists to finance my own enterprises by writing bankable business plans that demonstrated how my ventures met the needs of my funding sources. This book will enable you to greatly increase your chances for success.

In these pages, I will also impart my expertise as a business academician. Since 1992, I have been a professor at Baruch College of The City University of New York, the largest, most diverse business school in the United States, where I created and continue to teach both graduate and undergraduate courses on entrepreneurship and business plan development. As Academic Director of the Lawrence N. Field Center for Entrepreneurship at Baruch College, I have developed programs for entrepreneurs and have advised hundreds of individuals as they established their own ventures. All of my students and clients have learned to build their business plans on this single basic element of meeting their funders' needs. Now, you can learn how to follow this same route to creating a successful, effective, and bankable business plan.

Since my clients have an extremely broad range of business ideas—from New York City pedicabs to a web portal for Africans living away from their home countries—it's important for me to make the language I use to discuss the creation of a business plan as uniform as possible. No matter how you envision your eventual enterprise—as a store, an online service, or a firm that reaches your customers by mail order—I refer to the entity you're creating as your "company." When you start a business of any sort, you're establishing a means of delivering your product or service to a wider group of people. Even if you're setting yourself up as a sole practitioner, it's helpful to think of the way you organize your concept as a type of company with you at the helm making decisions and setting a course.

With my knowledge of what makes a successful business plan—from both the entrepreneur's and the funder's point of view—I can pass all the lessons I have learned along to you, the reader of *Bankable Business Plans*.

By following the process in this book you will guarantee that your individual business plan will be as bankable as possible.

Edward G. Rogoff
New York City
March 2007

PART I

THE POWER OF A BANKABLE BUSINESS PLAN

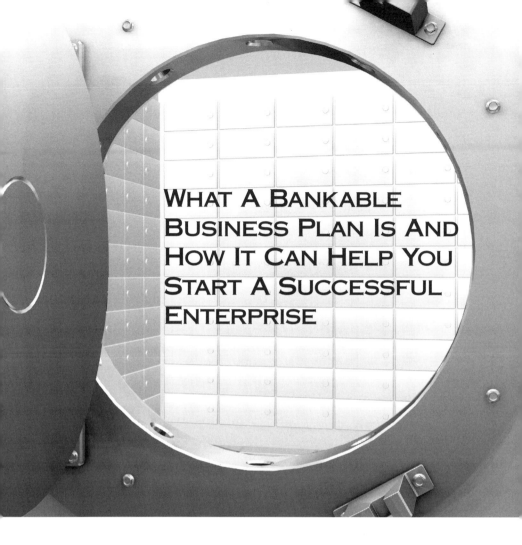

WHAT A BANKABLE BUSINESS PLAN IS AND HOW IT CAN HELP YOU START A SUCCESSFUL ENTERPRISE

When individuals come into the Lawrence N. Field Center for Entrepreneurship at Baruch College and sit down in my office, they usually open the conversation with one simple sentence: "I want to start my own business."

The next statement almost invariably includes one of the following four predicaments: "I have a specific idea for a business, but I don't know what to do next," or, "I know what I want to do and how I want to do it, but when I went to the bank for a loan, they said I had to show them something in writing before they would even talk to me," or, "I want to buy a business that I think I can make more successful, but I don't know how to start," or, "I'm an inventor and I've come up with a fabulous new product, but I don't have a clue how to get it manufactured—or sold."

The answer to all of these appeals for advice, whether the individual is opening a restaurant, taking over a competitor's ocarina manufacturing plant (an ocarina is a small, simple wind instrument), building a better mousetrap, selling a new kind of soap, or offering expert financial services to Wall Street investors is: "You need a business plan." Every one of these entrepreneurs is focused on a single goal: to build a successful enterprise that delivers profits and satisfaction to each owner. And no matter what that potential business is, there is one basic tool to employ in achieving that goal: a clear and compelling business plan.

Since I'm always interested in the types of businesses my clients want to develop into profitable and satisfying ventures, I ask them to tell me about their aspirations for the product or service they hope to provide. As they talk, I can sense their excitement and enthusiasm, even if they're uncertain about the next step. My job is to channel their passions into that next step: writing a strong business plan. And that's exactly what I am doing for you in this book.

Bankable Business Plans will help you create not only a strong business plan, but a bankable business plan—one that attracts financial support by meeting the needs of bankers, partners, and investors. By addressing the issues that are important to potential funders, you can convince them to believe in your concept because it will bring them success, as well as satisfaction to you. A bankable business plan is distinguished by certain characteristics: it serves a specific purpose, it doesn't follow formulas, it does follow good business thinking, it can be created regardless of your skills, it focuses on financial issues, and it can be used for starting, growing or buying a business.

Bankable Business Plans Serve A Specific Purpose

A good business plan is simply a document with a specific purpose. It *will*:

- Test the feasibility of your business idea.

- Determine the best financial resources to start your business through investors or partners.

- Secure enough debt by establishing loans, lines of credit, or payment terms.

- Identify the key people to work with you as employees, partners, or consultants.

- Establish business relationships with your customers, suppliers, or distributors.

- Create an operational template for the successful management of your business.

Most books and programs about creating business plans skip this step of defining the plan's main purpose, which results in plans that don't address the specific concerns of potential lenders, investors, or partners. *Bankable Business Plans* will enable you to define and accomplish this primary objective, while expressing your own confidence in your concept and attracting the support you need to start a new venture, grow your existing business, or purchase an established company.

Bankable Business Plans Don't Follow Formulas

Most books and software packages about creating business plans urge the reader to follow a template or copy an existing plan without first doing the conceptual work. This method produces a plan that sounds canned, generic, and lifeless, especially to someone who analyzes hundreds of proposals every month. It takes an experienced investor or lender about two seconds to spot a formula plan. Your business concept, and the work you accomplish to bring it to life, will make your plan compelling, and motivate others to support your efforts. *Bankable Business Plans* will show you how to create a unique, exciting, convincing, and thorough description of your proposed venture.

Bankable Business Plans Follow Good Business Thinking

Creating a business is a process that moves from conceptualization to implementation, and creating a business plan should follow the same sequence. Some books insist that the best way to begin a plan is to answer dozens of highly specific questions, which won't help if you haven't done the conceptual work first. Answering a question such as, "What is your profit goal for years one through five?" when you start to work on your plan, is rather like being asked to write a shopping list before you've decided what to cook. *Bankable Business Plans* takes you through the entire process from the conception of your initial idea, to testing it against basic criteria, to researching the market and the competition, to developing strategies, and, finally, to creating a plan for implementation. Since your resulting business plan will be based on the steps you took to create your business in your mind, it will be different from any other business plan—and it will be yours alone.

Bankable Business Plans Can Be Created Regardless of Your Skills

Many books and software packages assume that their readers are highly computer literate, with extensive knowledge of Windows, word processing, and spreadsheet programs. These are excellent skills to have and can save you tremendous amounts of time, but *Bankable Business Plans* is written for people at all skill levels. Although this book does not pretend to be an accounting text book, it will explain exactly what you need to learn and where you'll find the information to complete your financials. Reading this book is about creating a unique, effective business plan based on your enthusiasm for your venture and your willingness to learn about your industry. The only real skills you need to create a bankable business plan are your passion and your perseverance in learning how to do it effectively.

Bankable Business Plans Focus On Financial Issues

Most other books and programs simply ignore the fact that you're writing a document about an enterprise which, like all businesses, exists to make money. Since the people reading your plan will decide to invest in or lend money to your venture based largely on this document, your plan must address *their* issues. *Bankable Business Plans* not only takes you through the steps of producing quality financial projections, but tells you how to identify and satisfy specific concerns that matter to potential lenders and investors. Moreover, it is the only book that shows you how to make use of the *Risk Management Association* (RMA) data to establish your plan as credible. Since most bankers and many investors will compare your projections to the RMA data, knowing how to obtain and use these numbers is like being given the answer key to a test ahead of time.

Bankable Business Plans are for Starting, Growing, or Buying a Business

Whether you're starting a new business, growing an established business, or buying an existing business, you need to create a strong and bankable business plan. Even though the circumstances may vary and certain strategies and funding sources may be more effective than others, your basic business plan will still follow the same primary principles outlined in this book.

Your Business Plan Is An Extension Of You

Many entrepreneurs treat their business plans simply as a foot in the door, designed to elicit interest so the door opens wider. They assume that the plan will produce questions about issues not covered in the document, so reviewers will want to place a phone call or request an in-person meeting to get the answers. In my experience, this attitude is simply the rationalization of someone who is unwilling or unable to produce a quality plan.

Your plan speaks for you. If your plan is inadequate or unfocused, people will assume that you are inadequate and unfocused. If your written plan inspires more questions than positive comments during the initial reading by an executive or at a group discussion of your business concept, you can expect it to be added to the towering pile of rejects.

I am familiar with a mid-sized technology firm I'll call Duke's Photon Farm, which was founded by Duke Williams. Duke had been successful when technology-oriented firms attracted more money than there were places in which to invest it. When the love affair between the financial community and technology cooled, there were more deals than money to fund them, and Duke began to have trouble raising money.

Although he was both the CEO and the Chief Scientist of his business, Duke didn't want to answer questions from potential investors about his company's products or financial structure, including how much new investors could expect to earn from their investments. He produced what he called a business plan, but it was really only a general marketing document. It asserted that the company's products were great and that all Duke's Photon Farm needed to succeed was more money for marketing.

When Duke called to follow up, he was, predictably, asked about his company's products and financial situation and what new investors could expect to earn. But since Duke was both unwilling and unprepared to answer these questions, the discussions never led to the investments he needed. Investors were worried that Duke had something to hide, and since his business plan was inadequate, they felt that Duke was inadequate. After failing to raise the capital he needed to stay in business, Duke closed the barn doors on his Photon Farm, leaving many unhappy original investors, employees, and suppliers—none of whom had anything good to say about Duke or his farm.

Your plan must project who you are both explicitly and implicitly. By stating your background and qualifications, you are providing convincing reasons for others to consider your plan. By presenting a plan that is well organized, complete, easy to read, and persuasive, you are implying that you're the person who can make this business concept a success.

The Six Immutable Points

You can make certain that your business plan communicates your strengths by stressing what I call the *six immutable points*. When these six points are stated clearly and forcefully in your bankable business plan, your best qualities will be transmitted to the reader. The six immutable points are that:

1. You are profit oriented
2. You are honest
3. You are qualified
4. You are thorough
5. You are committed to meeting everyone's needs
6. You are flexible

Let's look at each of the six immutable points in greater detail, so you can make your business plan as bankable as possible:

1. You are profit oriented. Perhaps it sounds absurd to stress this goal. Isn't everyone profit oriented in the business world? Well, frankly, no. People have many reasons for wanting to start, buy, or build businesses, and profit is not always the most important goal. An entrepreneur may be driven by the desire to be her own boss, or to bring a needed product to the market. Entrepreneurs are also good at attracting people who will participate in the venture for reasons other than profit, such as to get needed experience when starting a new career. However, fundamentally, profit is what drives business and you need to make it clear that profit is your focus.

There are many examples of people who start medical research companies to find cures for diseases that afflict their family member or even a beloved pet. Investors would certainly be skeptical of a business plan for such a venture, wondering if profit were truly the founder's main motive. Funding sources may also be concerned that once the initial goal is met—in this case a cure—the founder's commitment to continue with the business and realize a profit will be negligible.

2. You are honest. If people participate in your plan by investing money, selling you raw materials, extending you credit, or becoming your employees, they need to know that you are honest. I have seen plans corrode people's reputations by leaving out key facts that are eventually uncovered, such as owning a previous business that failed, or by misrepresenting their credentials, such as claiming executive positions they held at a company when they really worked as mail sorters.

Lies are a particularly dangerous trap. I saw a business plan for a media company that listed the schools one of the partners attended and the degrees he earned. The only problem was that they were all fabrications. When one potential investor checked, as he did routinely, he discovered the lie and the plan quickly went into the trash.

Be candid and truthful about the information you present in your plan. Everyone has experienced some sort of failure, whether it's being fired from a job, training extensively for a profession you never entered, or starting a business that went belly up. Being honest about these issues and explaining how you learned an important lesson about yourself or running a business, almost always raises the esteem in which others will hold you.

3. You are qualified. The plan must demonstrate that you are qualified to undertake whatever the proposal requires. Many people feel that they need to possess all the qualifications themselves, but the business plan only needs to demonstrate that you are capable of identifying colleagues or becoming partners with others who have the technical knowledge you may lack. If you've been an airline pilot all your life, and want to open a restaurant that features squid-flavored pancakes, you must explain how you will compensate for this lack of experience, preferably by hiring a manager who has run a successful restaurant.

If your team is already in place, mention their qualifications along with yours. This will be presented briefly in a short, compelling argument for your concept, called an *executive summary*, more comprehensively in your business plan text and completely in your appendix, which should feature every résumé, including your own.

4. You are thorough. The plan must be comprehensive in your approach to your venture. In Part II, I've created Ten Essential Action Steps, which must be followed completely. Make a copy of the ten action steps and keep them next to your computer as you write your proposal. Don't skip any of these steps!

I recall seeing a plan for a chain of gyms that failed to mention how the owner would acquire the physical facilities in each community. When I asked about this missing piece, the entrepreneur said that he figured he'd go to a real estate agent in each town after he had raised his millions and was ready to open his facilities. Bad answer! Obtaining accurate real estate projections on both space availability and rental costs are critical steps in creating an effective business plan for a chain of gyms. This entrepreneur's omission may have been a sign of his inability to understand all the requirements of running a profitable business.

5. You are committed to meeting everyone's needs. Entrepreneurs have moral, ethical, legal, and self-interested reasons to treat everyone who participates in their enterprise fairly. There are contracts with the capital sources, as well as numerous legal requirements regarding the treatment of investors and employees. These include providing timely and complete financial statements, keeping the company current in all its taxes, and, of course, sharing profits according to the company's shareholder agreements. The plan must demonstrate that you are aware of these responsibilities, that you take them seriously, and will dispatch them fully.

I am familiar with the owner of an entertainment company, I'll call him Mr. Prince, who was brilliant, but scattered and disorganized. Mr. Prince raised a great deal of money because his plans made great sense and he was very smart. However, he never raised capital from the same source twice. Mr. Prince's disorganization prevented him from meeting the deadlines for providing financial statements to his investors and lenders, who liked his business, but refused to work with a company that didn't meet these basic requirements.

6. You are flexible. One of the fundamental challenges in writing a business plan is creating your executive summary and, at the same time, providing all the necessary details in your business plan text. In writing a business plan, you need to present yourself almost as a two-headed talent. Establishing and managing an enterprise are two very different tasks. You want to create an image of yourself as a founder who sees the mission of the organization in clear terms and who will not be deterred from reaching any goal. On the other hand, you must impress those evaluating your plan that you are also a boss who can carefully manage the day-to-day minutiae of running a business. You must demonstrate that you are flexible enough to adapt to any task that might come your way.

Since your ultimate success will depend more on your ability to manage the daily operations of your business, you must address this issue directly. Nothing speaks to these points more powerfully than previous experience. Even if you have never started your own ocarina-manufacturing company before, you may be an ocarina virtuoso who understands the instrument in all its manifest quirks, which would prepare you to judge manufacturing results. Or perhaps you were the leader of an internationally acclaimed ocarina orchestra, which demonstrates your ability to work with a number of colleagues, including finicky ocarina tuners as well as temperamental performing artists.

There is another reason to impress those reading your plan with your flexibility. As Jeff Bezos points out in his Foreword, the truth is that as soon as your business plan is written, it's probably already out of date. No matter what your industry is, your plan exists in a rapidly changing world and market. New competitors are emerging and old competitors are disappearing. Financial assumptions such as rents, raw materials, telecommunications services, and locations are all likely to change before your plan has been read by a potential investor. Even your own thinking may change regarding how your business should be positioned in the market once you have considered all the issues and completed your plan. You can deal with these changes by:

- Frequently updating and revising your plan.

- Welcoming the chance to revise, because each time you refine your plan, you are making it better.

- Keeping track of revisions by placing the date of each version on the cover page and the page headers.

Flexibility is often the key to business success. Bill Gates didn't start out to build a company that sold computer operating systems. He responded to a need that IBM expressed for a personal-computer operating system. John D. Rockefeller didn't plan to be an oil tycoon. He worked as a bookkeeper with a food wholesaler, then started his own food wholesaling firm. He saw a good opportunity in trading and the rest, as they say, is history. I am familiar with a logistics software company that began as a one-man trucking company, but that one man knew how to find opportunities and take advantage of them. Like these people, you—through your plan—must present yourself as someone who is flexible enough to respond to good opportunities.

Entrepreneurship Is A Team Sport

The definition of entrepreneurs that I like most is, "Entrepreneurs are business people who undertake ventures without regard to the resources under their direct control." Let's face it, limiting yourself to a venture you could do solely with your own resources—both human and financial—would probably result in a pretty small business. Your human resources would be confined to your own muscle and brain power during waking hours only, and your financial resources would be limited to your investments, retirement accounts, house, credit cards, cash in the bank, and those few treasured items, such as the original set of Batman comics that your uncle gave you when you were a kid.

Even if you are enormously wealthy, you probably wouldn't want to risk it all—especially the Batman comics—on your business idea. Assets of around $1 million are not likely to be enough to buy or start the business of your dreams. Most brand-name fast food franchises sell for more than that. Moreover, you need to be realistic and recognize the possibility that your business could fail and take all your assets with it.

Let's start with the assumption that, on the financial side, you are probably going to need help, either through loans from a family member, a friend, a bank, or a credit card company, or through investments from friends, family, business partners, or an investment group. Lenders let you borrow their money for a set period of time, and are paid interest along with receiving their loan amount, called principal, back in full. Investors buy equity or ownership shares in your business, and receive a share of the profits from operations or an eventual sale of the company.

As for the human resource side, do you really think you can operate your business completely alone? Very few businesses work that way. Consultants, freelancers, and individual investors may qualify as true one-man bands but, even for them, success (and sometimes failure) may spoil their solitude and require them to bring in employees or partners. And don't forget suppliers. The most solo operation still requires basic office supplies, such as paper and pencils. And absolutely no business operates without those important people, clients and customers.

No doubt about it, business is a team sport, requiring the contribution of others with different backgrounds, skills, and needs in order for you to build a successful venture, which brings me back to the definition I like and the reality that entrepreneurs must recruit and manage many resources—both human and financial—to create and grow a successful venture. This reality must be built into your business plan right from the beginning, which is why I believe that when you follow the process outlined in this book, you will create the most bankable business plan possible.

Starting a business and creating an effective business plan both require a great deal of thought before you set pen to paper or fingers to the computer keyboard. In Part II, I'll show you how each of the Ten Essential Action Steps will help you create a persuasive plan for your company.

PART II

The Ten
Essential
Action
Steps

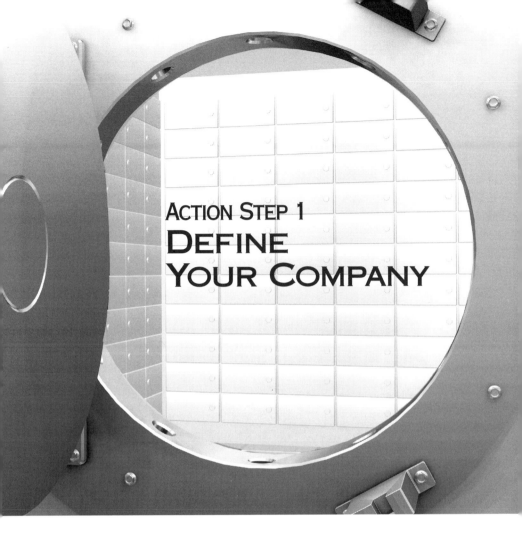

ACTION STEP 1
DEFINE YOUR COMPANY

WHAT WILL YOU ACCOMPLISH FOR OTHERS... AND YOURSELF?

Right from the start, you need to define your company in terms of what it will accomplish for others, including your customers, investors, lenders, suppliers, employees, and, of course, you. If you ask yourself about meeting the needs of each financial and human resource required to start and grow your venture, you will be well on your way to creating a bank-able business plan.

But first, write down all the personal needs your company will satisfy. In the privacy of my office, you can tell me about these highly individual reasons you have for starting a business:

escaping an overbearing boss, not being able to get along with colleagues you didn't hire yourself, or proving to your skeptical father-in-law that you can be a success.

Then, set these incentives aside. They may inspire you, but they will have no place in your final business plan. Your personal reasons for starting your business are not of particular interest to the potential investors or funders, who will be reading and analyzing the effectiveness of your concept.

Even if you're eager to start a company that can find a cure for the rare disease that made the feathers on your beloved parakeet fall out, your personal motivation will be of little or no significance to the funding sources whose support you need. Potential investors need to know that your business will be meaningful and marketable to enough people who can use your product or service in order to earn a profit. Your deep-seated desire to find a cure so that your parakeet can grow new feathers, may galvanize you to become a tireless crusader but, unless there is a commercial and profitable application for the product you hope to develop, your emotional commitment won't mean much to investors. In fact, they may worry about your continued commitment to the cause, if a cure isn't found in time to work wonders on your particular ailing pet.

Concentrate on the external needs your company will meet. What will your product or service enable people to do better, more cheaply, more safely, or more efficiently? Will your restaurant make people's palates delirious with new taste sensations? Will your new mousetrap help people capture mice without feeling sick to their stomachs? Will your new bubble gum scented bubble bath revolutionize the way children agree to take nightly baths? Will the cure for your featherless parakeet also work for the thousands of pets who lose their fur, as well.

Think of all the positive benefits your company will provide. Write them down. Admire them. Absorb them into your consciousness. Believe in them. These are the primary motivators that readers of your business plan will respect and value.

What Will Your Business Accomplish For Your Customers?

Your customers are your only source of revenue. Why will they spend their money on your product or service, and why will they return to spend money again? Unless there are strong answers to these questions, your business plan will not make it to first base.

Suppose you're planning to open a pet supply store in your town. People with pets are obviously buying the food, supplies, treats, and other items at some store in the community, so, why will they want to shop at your place? Will your service be better? Your location more convenient? Your prices lower? Your selection greater? Your hours of operation longer? Your delivery faster and cheaper? Will your store be more fun, a pleasanter place to shop? Unless some of the answers to these and other questions are yes, then you won't be accomplishing enough for your customers to build the large and loyal group of shoppers you'll need to operate a successful pet store.

Sometimes, a business is successful simply because demand is greater than the supply. I had a client at the Field Center who wanted to open a day care center for preschoolers. Her analysis was quite simple: She knew a dozen families that were having trouble finding day care facilities for their children in their neighborhood. She figured that the demand was there and was woefully under served. She didn't have to be better or cheaper than her competition. She just had to be in business. She was right, and opened a day care center that was successful from its first day of operation.

What Will Your Business Accomplish For Your Investors?

Investors are the people or firms that buy stock in your company. Owning stock entitles them to a share of the profits either from general operations or from the sale of your business. Keep in mind that investors have many options. They can buy very secure government bonds, or publicly traded stocks; they can purchase real estate, or invest in any number of large or small businesses other than your own.

Entrepreneurs have an uphill struggle to attract investors, because these other options offer attractive returns and, probably, less risk. Investing in smaller businesses is chancier than buying stocks in large, publicly traded, well-established, and well-financed companies with a long history of profitability. In addition, those companies' stocks are defined as being *highly liquid*, meaning they can be sold at virtually any point very quickly to raise cash or to change investments. Most investments in startups or smaller entrepreneurial ventures are highly *illiquid*, meaning the investors' money is locked into the company's operating expenses until the business raises additional financing, becomes profitable enough to buy them out, or is sold.

To attract investors in the face of this risk and lack of liquidity, entrepreneurs must offer the potential of very high returns. How high? Well, it's not unusual for investors to expect credible and reasonable projections in the range of 20 percent to 30 percent annual returns before they will buy stock in your company. At this early stage in planning your business, you don't have the detailed financial projections that you will eventually need to show investors, but you can produce some back-of-the-envelope calculations to assure yourself that this rate of return is possible.

Suppose you're thinking of raising money to invest in real estate. It's not unusual for a bank to lend 80 percent or more of the purchase price. If the property you're considering makes a profit of $100,000 per year and you expect to pay ten times that profit, or $1 million to purchase the property, you will need $800,000 from a bank and the remaining $200,000 from investors. If you expect to increase profits to $150,000 per year within three years by raising rents when old leases come up for renewal, then your building will be worth $1.5 million, and the investors' $200,000 will be worth $700,000. That is more than a 50 percent annual return, and should be enough to make any investor happy.

Of course, there are additional considerations I haven't mentioned yet, such as transaction charges, lawyer's fees, your share of the profits for finding and managing the deal, and the need to spend money repairing the building you want to buy. But, for this stage, you have at least shown that high, attractive returns are possible and you should continue to work out the details.

Many entrepreneurs think they can attract investment for reasons other than financial returns. Your family and friends may simply want to help you start or build your business because they like you and believe in your talent. It is also possible that your business may serve a societal good, such as supporting medical research or helping endangered wildlife. I know this kind of investing does take place. I've actually seen it happen a few times, but my advice to clients is *don't count on it*. Most investors interested in such causes still want to see high projected returns, too. If your plan can't produce significant returns for investors, then perhaps you should change from starting a business to establishing a charity or foundation. A not-for-profit organization may be a more accurate description of what you're trying to accomplish, and there is certainly nothing wrong with that!

What Will Your Business Accomplish For Your Lenders?

Lenders, such as banks, provide your company with debt financing through loans in exchange for which they are paid interest. Because interest rates are generally far lower than the returns expected by most investors who buy stock in your company, lenders require much greater certainty that their principal will be returned and their interest paid. For this reason, lenders are always repaid completely before investors can receive a single penny. Business loans currently have interest rates in the 8 to 13 percent range, depending on the borrower's record, and the amount being borrowed.

To increase the likelihood that lenders will not lose their principal, they usually ask for *security*, which is a claim on an asset they can seize and sell in the event of a payment default. We are all familiar with the concept of a bank foreclosing on a house if the homeowner falls behind on mortgage payments. The same concept applies to business loans; only the security may be tied to an actual business asset such as inventory, receivables, equipment, buildings, or land.

The federal government provides guarantees to small business loans made by banks through the Small Business Administration (SBA). The purpose of this program is to encourage banks to make loans to small and new businesses, because small businesses create most new jobs and generate a large share of overall economic growth. SBA guarantees cover between fifty and eighty-five percent of the total business loan, depending on the loan amount and the program type.

Most banks and other lenders require that business owners also provide a personal guarantee for the repayment of a loan. This means that, in the case of default, the bank can claim these personally owned assets, such as a house, as repayment of the loan. Offering a personal guarantee is a very serious step for an entrepreneur, because lenders will do whatever they have to do to be repaid. I have seen sad cases of people, some of them very wealthy, who lost a large share of their personal assets to banks after signing personal guarantees on a business venture before thinking through the consequences.

Remember, lenders always want multiple assurances that they will be paid their interest and principal. First, they will look to the profits of your business for repayment, then to the business's assets, and, finally, to you personally. If your business plan can demonstrate that all these sources of repayment are likely, you have a good chance of garnering support from lenders.

What Will Your Business Accomplish For Your Suppliers?

Most businesses rely on purchasing goods to resell or to use in manufacturing other products. The companies that sell these inputs to your business are your suppliers, and they are essential. If you want to open a tea shop, you had best check to make sure that the supply of distinctive teas you'll need is actually available at a price that you can afford. If you're planning to open an architectural design firm, you probably need special-ized computer and software systems to lease or purchase.

Suppliers, of course, view you and your fledgling business as a new customer. And every business loves new customers. Right? Well, maybe. Before a computer company installs a very expensive system in your office, they are going to want some of the same assurances a bank requires before making a loan, namely that they will be paid in full or get their computers back. Before a supplier delivers thousands of dollars worth of tea for your shop, she will certainly want to be paid up front, since most consumable goods are not returnable. Over time, as you prove your creditworthiness with your suppliers, they will likely extend you credit, just as you may eventually offer credit to your faithful customers.

This is an issue worth exploring right at the beginning of designing your business. I have seen a private medical office stymied by its failure to obtain essential testing equipment because the supplier didn't want to aggravate its larger client, a nearby hospital. I saw a high-tech manufacturing business fail over some crucial raw materials that simply couldn't be bought, because they were going to the supplier's larger, more established customers.

What Will Your Business Accomplish For Your Employees?

If your venture requires employees—and almost all do—your business plan needs to demonstrate that you have the means to attract and keep people who have the right qualifications and abil-ities. If you feel certain that you will always be able to hire good employees at the right price in sufficient numbers, think again.

I witnessed a business close down that provided telephone customer support to software companies because they were lo-cated in a city without an adequate supply of well-educated, com-puter-literate people to hire. I have seen restaurants built, but never open, in communities where the owners simply could not recruit a full-fledged staff of cooks, busboys, and waitstaff.

Then, there were the companies with large enough pools of qualified employees, who couldn't afford to match the excellent salaries and benefits offered by their competitors, so they were forced to close down. I have seen several businesses with such poor management reputations that they could only hire people who couldn't get jobs elsewhere. Needless to say, these businesses always underperformed their competition, until they failed or were sold to owners who hired entirely new management teams.

Your bankable business plan must define the types of employees you need and demonstrate that you will be able to hire and retain them. Employees want fair pay, a good place to work, and opportunities for the future. If your budget calls for salaries at market rates or better and you can show what similar businesses are paying for similarly qualified employees, then you have established your ability to hire a good staff. Creating a good place to work depends on you and your management team. Have you managed a staff successfully before? Were your workers satisfied, as evidenced by low turnover rates? Do some of your previous employees want to come work for you again? Positive answers to these questions will indicate that you can provide an attractive work environment.

Opportunities for employees in entrepreneurial ventures arise from two sources: growth and strong management. If your company is growing, there will be opportunities for promoting employees into positions with more clout and pay. Strong management feels secure enough to give its employees the chance to learn different tasks and build new skills. Discussing these issues in your business plan and demonstrating a record that you understand both sources of opportunities for employees, indicates that your company will work as much for its employees as its employees will work for you.

Last, And Perhaps Least, What Will Your Business Accomplish For You?

If you have demonstrated that you can meet the needs of the key groups you must recruit to build a successful business, then you will learn what the business is capable of accomplishing for you. For most aspiring business owners, prime personal goals include being their own bosses, working at what they enjoy doing, gaining a sense of accomplishment by building a business, and creating the opportunity to make money.

You may be wondering why I didn't mention money first. The answer is that virtually every study of business owners shows that making money, while an important ambition, is rarely the most compelling goal of an entrepreneur. For example, people in family-owned businesses frequently list spending time with their relatives and employing family members as their most important goals.

Of course, your goals are unique to you. However, to establish them in your own mind, you need to do three things:

1. State your personal goals. They may be some of the ambitions listed here, or they may be issues such as having the opportunity to travel, work with children, or get away from incompetent bosses you've worked for in the past. Make these personal goals into a list.

2. Ask yourself whether your business will accomplish those goals. Aspiring business owners who ask themselves this question honestly, often realize that their business idea will not produce the fast path to the riches they envisioned. Or that their dream of doing creative work most of the day dissolves as the reality of running a business—selling to clients, keeping the books, or training a new assistant—comes into play. If the way you have defined your business does, in fact, accomplish your goals, then you can move on to the third step.

3. Tear up the personal goals list you just made! From here on your task is to convince others that your business will meet *their* needs and that they should contribute *their* time, money, or expertise to become your investors, lenders, customers, suppliers, or employees.

If you have been able to define your company in terms of what it will do for others, then you have also defined a worthy and potentially successful business concept. But, beware. As we work through the process of creating a bankable business plan, you may find truth to the expression, "The devil's in the details." Issues and problems may arise that cause you to return to this step of defining a new concept, and force you to start over again.

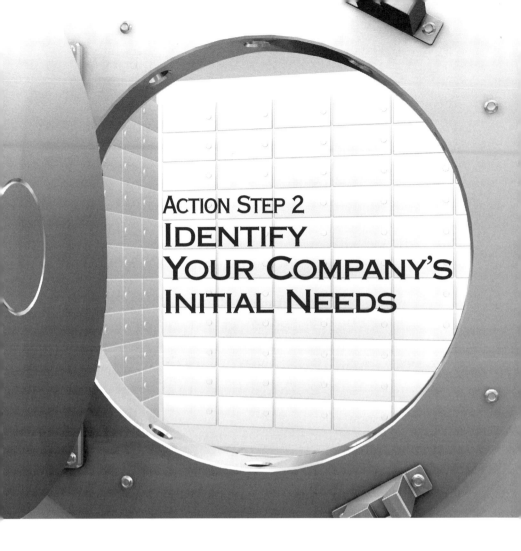

ACTION STEP 2
IDENTIFY YOUR COMPANY'S INITIAL NEEDS

WHAT WILL YOU REQUIRE TO GET STARTED?

Whether you want to buy an existing company with 300 employees, or can start your business by only adding an extra phone line to your home-office desk, you need to make a list of the materials you'll require. Some may be tangible, such as 500 file folders and a large cabinet in which to store them all. Other requirements may be intangible, such as time to create a product design or to do market research. You may need to hire an assistant to develop a retrievable filing system for the 500 folders, or hire a consultant to set up a computer system that may be beyond your technical skills.

If you're going to build a better mousetrap, you may have constructed a prototype out of used toothpaste tubes and bent paper clips at home, but you'll need a sturdier, more attractive model to show potential investors. What exactly will your mousetrap look like? What materials will you need? Do you require money for research and development to improve on your original toothpaste tube and paper clip construction? Do you need to hire an engineer to draw up accurate manufacturing designs? Should you patent your invention? Will you need to investigate federal safety standards for mousetraps? Should you allow time to test the materials for durability before you start manufacturing thousands of mousetraps? How many mousetraps do you plan to make at first? The answers to these questions will become the budget line items in your list of startup costs for your business.

And, if you want to open a restaurant, you'll have to figure out how much money you'll need to cover your rent, equipment, and renovations before you start turning a profit. If you're the bubble bath manufacturer, you may need to purchase specialized software to stamp bar codes on every bottle. If you're the financial-services company entrepreneur, you need a financial model of the business to show potential investors.

Next, do your homework. Call a real estate broker and look at actual spaces in the neighborhood in which you'd like to establish your business. Make a chart of the most expensive and least expensive sites by location and square footage. Then, estimate how much space you require and how much money you'll need to allow for rent.

In the mousetrap scenario, you should contact an engineer who can help you create design specifications. Be sure to ask about her fee structure. Will she charge by the job or by the hour? Will you own the designs or will she? And, if you're the client who wants to make bath time fun, check to see if bubble gum fragrance for your kiddie bubble bath soap is readily available or has to be manufactured from scratch. How much fragrance will you have to buy to make your soap smell yummy? And, if you're the entrepreneur who wants to open a financial services firm, find out what a half-page ad in *The Wall Street Journal* costs. (Hint: it's mind boggling!)

Make a list of all the tangible and intangible resources you need to get your business going. The total estimated price of all of these items will become your startup cost whether you're buying more toothpaste tubes, an ocarina factory, or simply installing a new telephone line on your desk. If there's any item in your estimates that seems unreasonably high (the *Wall Street Journal* ad is a likely culprit), research alternatives. Keep in mind that it's better to include every element you truly need along with a reasonable estimate of the cost of each item, so you don't run out of money or default on your loans. Be honest and conservative in your estimates, but be optimistic, too.

Whether you are starting a business completely from scratch or buying an existing business with hundreds of employees and millions of dollars in revenue, completing this step carefully and diligently is important, because it starts the process of quantifying what you will need. You can think of this step as the first cut at researching and enumerating the resources your business will require. When you have completed the entire process, which is still a few steps away, you will have produced detailed, credible, and compelling <u>financial projections</u>.

Now, it is time to make your resource list more specific and begin your research into each item. If you are planning to purchase an existing, operating business, you will probably have an easier time with this analysis of your initial needs. Existing businesses have actual numbers for costs, so research is considerably easier.

However, even for existing businesses it is valuable to review all categories of expenses in detail to determine where you might be able to reduce costs. For example, if you are purchasing a restaurant, you might be able to improve on the prices or terms by changing suppliers. You may also devise a more effective way to advertise and promote the restaurant. While you do have real numbers to work from when you buy an existing business, you still must research the financial figures thoroughly.

For startup businesses, few operational parameters are established, so the number of options to consider may be very large. For example, suppose a group of accountants wants to start a new firm. They probably have a geographic area in mind, based on whom their initial clients are likely to be. Even so, there might be multiple towns or counties to check for possible office space. They need to research the tax laws in each town or county (not a difficult task for accountants!) because these could make a significant difference in their costs. They should talk to businesspeople in the area to find out which locations are regarded as high status and which as low status.

Some new businesses can locate almost anywhere on earth. If you're starting a clothing factory, you might want to consider as many countries as possible to uncover the best shipping rates, labor costs, and tax breaks. You might want to engage a location consultant for guidance, in which case you should explore various options and costs for these services.

By now, you're probably realizing that you will be spending less time with your feet up on your desk thinking conceptually and making grand plans, and more time slogging through the details of your options. At least I warned you.

The Major Expenses

There is no better way to develop expense estimates than to actually go shopping, so, if you like to shop, you'll enjoy this step. In many industries there is often a big gap between asking price and final price, so shopping may reveal realistic prices. For other types of expenses, such as raw materials, data, or skilled workers, obtaining realistic cost estimates can be a challenge.

Your major expenses will consist of:

- **Real estate**
- **Employees and employee benefits**
- **Startup and capital costs**
- **Advertising and promotion**

Let's look at each of these expenses in detail.

Real Estate. One industry that often has a large gap between bid and asking price is real estate. If you're examining real estate costs, start with newspaper ads, but don't stop there. Call agents and go see available spaces. Discuss what a final price is likely to – be. In real estate, as in many other industries, you can never know what price someone will actually accept until you put a firm offer on the table, so ask about other locations and recent deals. This is a time-consuming and sometimes tedious process, but it will pay dividends in a better final deal. After you have seen a number of properties and talked with several agents, you will understand pricing and the trade-offs on location and amenities.

Employees and employee benefits. For most businesses, salary and benefit costs are a major expense. Your ability to find and retain quality employees can be one of the major determinants of your ability to deliver a quality product or service to your customers. This is another estimate you cannot trust to winging it. To obtain accurate salary estimates, you need to talk with employment agencies, employees who do similar jobs at other companies, and managers of companies who handle hiring. You can also try some simulated hiring. By this, I mean you could actually advertise positions for a company that expects to open soon and have people apply for the jobs. From the response you receive, the quality of the people who apply, and the conversations you have with the applicants, you will be able to develop real, bankable knowledge of likely employment costs and availability.

Employee benefits include private health insurance, pension plans, stock-option plans, life insurance and government programs such as Social Security and Worker's Compensation. This is a very technical, complex, and highly regulated area, which may make it difficult for you to estimate these costs. The alternative is to ask a benefits consultant, a financial planner, or an accountant to give you some guidance. You need to decide what benefits you'll offer and how the costs will be divided between the company and the employees. If you're hiring people who view their jobs as temporary before they move on to better positions, like fast food employees, then it's best to provide minimal benefits and make their current pay as high as possible. If you're hiring people who see their jobs as long-term career moves, then you should offer long-term benefits, such as pension plans and stock options. Analyzing this expense will enable you to compile a description of the benefits you expect to offer and a cost per employee expressed as a percentage of each salary, a fixed amount per employee, or a combination of the two.

Startup and capital costs. Startup and capital costs for items such as restaurant equipment, filing cabinets, or raw materials for manufacturing, are very dependent on the exact nature of your business. Establishing a metal fabricating company is going to have very different startup and capital requirements from creating a home-based computer consulting business. Whatever the precise list of startup costs, get bids and speak with as many potential sources as possible.

Advertising and promotion. For many new and established retail businesses, advertising is an important part of the initial plan to attract new or additional customers. Action Step 5 describes a marketing campaign in detail, but in order to establish what you need in an initial burst of advertising, you must consider two issues. First, where will you find your customers? Do they read particular magazines or newspapers, or listen to certain radio stations? Can you purchase a list of likely customers? The answers to these questions will help you create a basic budget for reaching your market. The second issue to consider is that repetition is the essence of advertising. You will need to purchase multiple ads, send multiple mailings, and make multiple sales calls before your message is heard by a large share of your target audience. Be certain to budget enough funds to achieve this critically important repetition.

Once you've identified your company's initial requirements, you will have a much clearer concept of what you'll need to buy, invest, or borrow in order to start your business. This information will become the basis for the credible financial analysis that will be an essential component of your bankable business plan.

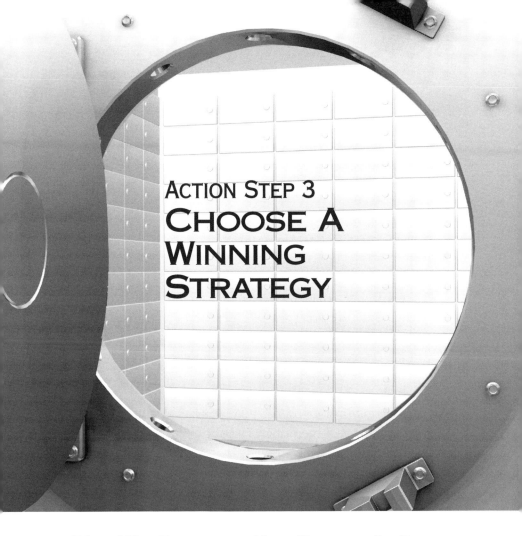

Action Step 3
Choose A Winning Strategy

What Will Distinguish Your Product Or Service From Your Competition?

Now it is time to select an effective business strategy for your enterprise, based on your specific business goals. Before you can decide on a winning strategy, however, you have to know what you want to achieve with your concept, such as positive cash flow, personal wealth, profitability, improved market share, or an advantageous sale of an existing business. Strategy is *how* you will accomplish those goals through actions such as advertising and cost control, as well as product characteristics and quality.

This chapter takes you through the process of creating a winning strategy for your business by helping you to understand your industry, define your competitive advantage, and analyze your business' strengths and weaknesses. You will learn that vague strategies, such as "I will have the best product available," are not nearly as powerful, convincing, or successful as specific strategies.

Here are some important points to remember about strategies. They are:

- generally outwardly focused, influencing how your business will interact with its external environment including your customers, competitors, suppliers, and the government.

- about how your company will achieve a strong and long-lasting position in the marketplace, or competitive advantage, which is key to your ability to attract customers or to price products that earn a profit.

- specific, simple to implement, and based on reasonable assumptions.

- a blueprint for building the results you want.

Create A Powerful Competitive Advantage

There are two fundamental categories of business strategies: *Low-Cost Leadership* and *Differentiation*. Choosing the best strategies from within these two categories is the first step in developing a strong competitive advantage for your business. Once you understand these two basic categories, you can adapt the best strategies to your business according to the type of industry you have chosen.

Low-Cost Leadership

Everyone likes to pay the lowest possible price for any product or service, so companies that can offer customers the lowest prices have a strong competitive advantage. Masters of low-cost strategies include WalMart, which uses its enormous buying power to negotiate lower prices from its suppliers, then manages store operations so efficiently that it can price below its competitors and still make a profit. Dell Computer, regarded as the most efficient manufacturer of personal computers, employs a strategy that allows the company to increase market share by lowering prices, while still remaining profitable and forcing its competitors to lose money if they try to match Dell's prices. Toyota has accomplished the same low-cost leadership in the auto industry.

Many entrepreneurs starting new businesses think they will be able to execute a low cost strategy, but most find out otherwise. It is difficult for a new business to operate more efficiently than existing businesses that are already known to their market, are profitable, and have experienced and knowledgeable staff. Existing businesses usually have access to more financing than startups, giving them a big advantage if a price war breaks out.

Differentiation

Designing your product or service precisely to match the preferences of your customers makes your business attractive, and sets it apart from your competitors. Think about the choices you have when you decide to book a hotel room. Hotel companies differentiate themselves with such qualities as room size, location, luxurious appointments, reputation, sports facilities, image, price, and level of service.

Motel 6, for example, is geared to the bargain traveler who isn't interested in amenities, but the company is successful because they've designed their product to appeal to a sizable, yet very specific, group of customers. Your business plan needs to define your target market and state how you will differentiate your product or service to appeal to your potential customers.

To be successful, every business must have some competitive advantage over its competition. Competition is the enemy of profits: It's great for customers, but bad for business. Competitive advantage is the barrier that keeps competition at bay. The stronger your competitive advantage, the more profitable and less affected by competition your business is likely to be.

The first step in selecting strategies from one of the two basic categories—either low-cost leadership or differentiation—is to identify a competitive advantage for your product or service. How will you establish that your product or service is better, cheaper, more delicious or more convenient? How can you make your company more noticeable than your competitors? What restraints in your business or industry might determine which strategy you choose?

Your competitive advantage may include designing special features not found in rival products. It may entail superior service characteristics such as speedier delivery, a lower price, or more attentive salespeople. Perhaps you're establishing an image or brand of exceptional quality or reputation. Does your product or service bestow a certain status on its users? Does it create more profits or other benefits for your customers' own endeavors?

Imagine you're that pilot who wants to open a restaurant that serves squid-flavored pancakes. What will your competitive advantage be? Do you know that the people in the neighborhood devour other squid-based dishes and can't seem to get their fill? Have all the other pancake restaurants in the community failed to include squid-flavored items on their menus? Is squid much cheaper to acquire than other more traditional pancake ingredients, such as bananas? Will the decor of your restaurant be so enticing to squid lovers that they'll come in to look around and then discover how delicious your squid pancakes can be?

Perhaps you want to position your mousetrap for a primarily upscale market because the best design requires titanium, and manufacturing costs will be so expensive only rich people will be able to afford your product. Maybe the mousetrap is so fantastically effective that wealthy people will want hundreds of them around their vast country estates and polo-pony barns.

Examples of strong competitive advantages include:

A patent, which prevents anyone else from using your product without your permission. Pharmaceuticals are protected by patents for significant periods of time, making them both high priced and highly profitable.

A government-granted monopoly, such as a cable-television franchise, which prevents anyone else from entering the same business in your particular territory.

An effective monopoly, such as Microsoft and Windows operating systems, that is protected by copyrights. Microsoft also has a competitive advantage by its emergence as the *de facto* standard in personal computers, virtually assuring that purchasers of new computers will want Windows.

A great name brand, such as Jell-O or Oreo cookies, gives a company a prime position in people's minds within that product category. Many small, but long-established businesses also have very strong brand names, such as local restaurants, banks, and bookstores.

Speed is a powerful competitive advantage. From the days of clipper ships to FedEx jets, customers have always valued speed. Other businesses built with speed as a key competitive advantage include Domino's Pizza, Dell Computer, and any company that uses Web and e-mail applications.

Some businesses have inherently weak competitive advantages. Electronics or appliance retailers, which sell the same products as their competitors, are often forced to compete solely on price and a reputation for service. There are exceptions, however. In New York City, there are thousands of takeout pizzerias, often located within a block or less of each other, yet they all manage to be successful because there is lots of demand for pizza, the stores are easy to operate, and customers usually opt for convenience in choosing which pizzeria to patronize.

Here are the principal strategies you can use with somewhat weaker competitive advantages to make your business profitable:

Lower your price. If you can sell the same products or services as your competitors at a lower price, you will attract customers. However, can you undercut your competitors' prices and still make a profit? You can if your costs are lower than theirs, so the key to this strategy is having an operating plan that makes you more efficient, or able to purchase materials from suppliers or manufacturers at a lower cost than your competitors. This strategy has worked for WalMart, but has failed for the dozens of electronics retailers who have gone out of business because of their inability to match or beat their competitors' prices and still make a profit. Remember my warning—this is a tough strategy to execute.

Provide great service. The differences in service levels are often the deciding factor for customers. A reputation for service will often influence a customer's choice of independent contractors, such as plumbers or electricians. Car dealers make little or no money on new car sales because all dealers of any particular manufacturer sell the same models. They usually end up competing based on post-sale services, such as regular maintenance, lending cars to customers during repairs, or offering a pick-up and drop-off service. Dealers often have local reputations that are well known, plus the car manufacturers rate each dealer's service record. Most car buyers would rather pay more for a car from a dealer with a good service reputation, whether they purchase new cars on a regular basis or keep a car for years.

Build a positive image and brand. Most buyers feel that the brands of the products they buy or the companies they do business with reflect their values, while also sending a message about themselves to friends and associates.

Develop a good reputation. Nothing is more reassuring to a customer than buying from a company or person with a strong reputation. Customers often suffer *buyer's remorse* after making a major purchase, a period of insecurity in which they wonder if the cost was worth the price of ownership. This is when they need the reassurance of knowing they bought the product from a person or company of high reputation or with a strong name brand. A solid reputation is not only a selling point in its own right, but it actually immunizes customers from a bad case of buyer's remorse. Having a strong reputation is a great competitive advantage.

Achieve high status. We all know that Rolex, Rolls Royce, and Burberry are status consumer products. For customers who want the status these products impart, there are few competitors and, almost by definition, a higher price to pay. That's why status is such a desirable competitive advantage.

I have a friend who owned a very expensive Lexus, which is manufactured by Toyota. When he traded it in a couple of years later, during leaner times, for a Toyota Camry, I asked him what the difference was between the two cars. "Twenty thousand dollars and a lot of status with my friends," was his reply! If your plan includes positioning your product or service as high status, then your business can expect to have higher-than-average profit margins.

Use A SWOT Analysis To Determine The Competitive Advantage Of An Existing Business

A good way to begin your research into competitive advantage is with a SWOT analysis, an acronym which stands for Strengths, Weaknesses, Opportunities, and Threats. You can even do a SWOT analysis for a startup, if you are brutally frank about where your company will stand relative to existing businesses in your market. Let's look at each of the elements of a SWOT analysis:

Strengths include the organization's internal capabilities, such as good relationships with key customers, or strong technical skills.

Weaknesses also include such internal disadvantages as inadequate warehouse facilities or poor sales staff.

Opportunities relate to external issues such as under-served markets in an adjacent community, or a current competitor who could be bought out.

Threats are also external to the business and include such problems as an official change in traffic patterns that could make it more difficult for customers to find the store, or a potential increase in sales taxes that could send customers across the border to an adjacent state.

Your SWOT analysis does not have to be scientific or particularly rigorous, but it will help you organize your thoughts about the strategic position of an existing business. Addressing how you will cope with any problems you uncover in your SWOT analysis will give your business plan credibility. Investors and lenders expect startups, as well as existing businesses, to have weaknesses or threats, but they also expect your plan to indicate how you will manage these potential difficulties and minimize their impact.

Plan Ahead: Anticipate An Exit Strategy

You need to give extensive thought to how you will exit your business—and create profits for yourself and your investors. Some businesses, such as real estate, have assets with clear values that are relatively easy to realize through sales, and can produce quick exits. Other businesses, such as consulting companies, have assets which are based on the owner's expertise and the relationships between staff members and clients, and are much more difficult to value or exit.

Whatever your business, you need to craft an exit strategy in advance and build it into your financial projections. Potential investors are going to ask you about it, because they probably don't see themselves staying with you forever, and are focused on how much they will earn. Lenders want to be sure that any sale of your company will produce enough money to pay them back in full, plus interest.

Match Your Strategies To Any Type Of Industry

Many people believe that only ventures in rapidly growing industries can be successful. In fact, you can build a successful business in any type of industry and in virtually any competitive environment—if you use the right strategy. Investors and lenders recognize these five industry categories:

- **Emerging**
- **Maturing**
- **Stagnant and Declining**
- **Fragmented**
- **Industries with Dominant Leaders**

Let's review the nature of these five categories and the specific strategies that are likely to lead to success in each.

Emerging Industries

Emerging industries are the "Gold Rush" opportunities that spring up quickly and attract a great deal of attention and investment in the early phases of their development. Examples include the Internet in the 1990s, housing construction immediately following World War II and the film industry after the invention of the moving-picture camera. While there was tremendous growth in each of these industries, it was also encumbered by a great deal of competition and uncertainty. Let's look at the pluses and minuses of doing business in an emerging industry:

Pluses of Emerging Industries

A rapid rate of growth of new customers.

Easy entrance to the market, even for people without experience, because no one has experience.

Lack of established industry leaders who need to be overcome, making the playing field rather level for all competitors.

Minuses of Emerging Industries

Many of the technologies and standards are unclear and may not be clarified for a long time. If you owned a software company early in the personal computer revolution, it was not apparent which operating system would become dominant. If you decided to write your software for an operating system other than Microsoft's, then you probably put yourself out of business. Similar struggles exist today regarding the digital distribution systems for music, books, and cellular phones.

The ease of entering the market can be a substantial negative if you've established *your* company first. For example, the low barriers to entry in the website design business have reduced profit margins as new companies and individuals launch their ventures and underprice their services to build revenue and a customer base.

Lack of information about your competition can prevent you from making sound business decisions. If you can't figure out who your competitors are, what products they're developing, or how they're advertising and pricing their merchandise or services, you'll be operating in a fog. As a result, you may not realize that your market is too limited and your price too high to attract customers until it's too late and your business fails.

Buyers may delay purchasing products in an emerging industry because they want to see if a dominant technology arises or if prices will drop dramatically as manufacturing costs become less expensive. You have probably done this yourself. Maybe you didn't buy a VCR player until you were confident which of the competing systems would capture the market, or you waited until prices were lowered and quality improved. This reluctance on the part of buyers to purchase a new product immediately can spell major problems for entrepreneurs in emerging industries.

Necessary resources for emerging industries can be hard to find, and you may have to pay more to procure them. During the California gold rush of 1849, there were reports of prospectors paying more than $100 for a shovel that used to cost only 50 cents. During the peak of the Internet boom, high school students who could program in HTML, the language used for websites, were being offered jobs at website design companies for $100,000 per year. It is often better to sell *to* companies in emerging industries than to be one! Otherwise, resources such as financing, components, and raw materials will be expensive, if available at all.

The Best Strategies for Emerging Industries

Create a bold, win-early strategy. This is the approach that Amazon.com and 3Com, the maker of the Palm Pilot, have used in their emerging industries. Grow as quickly as possible to make yourself the brand name that customers know.

Be the best. Sony, Hewlett-Packard, and Cisco Systems are companies that established performance standards for their new products, putting distance between themselves and their competitors.

Superserve niche markets. Define and develop customer groups by geography, application, pricing, or marketing. Computer Associates owns many niche software products, such as computer security and accounting software. It doesn't compete with the big players, but it finds and serves markets that are too small to interest giants like Microsoft.

Pick the winning technology as soon as possible. If you had owned a company that produced videotapes when the Betamax format was still battling with VHS for dominance, you had to switch to VHS as soon as it became clear that VHS was becoming the market standard. If you didn't act quickly, you would have wasted money on a rapidly disappearing market.

Build brand loyalty, especially with consumer products. Given all the competition and uncertainty in emerging markets, the quicker you can build a brand that customers can believe in, the sooner you will be constructing some protection from your competitors. Brands are a powerful tool for grabbing and keeping customers.

Businesses in emerging industries need to be prepared for well-financed outsiders to move in aggressively. Microsoft has systematically cornered the word processing, e-mail, spreadsheet, and database software markets, often destroying all competition in its path. Entertainment giants such as AOL Time Warner, Disney, and Viacom had the stability and finances to wait for the cable television industry to develop into a large scale, viable business from thousands of small, local operators and minor programming firms before they set out to absorb them profitably. Today, these large companies dominate their industry.

If your business is in an emerging, high-growth industry, you should think about what happens to your venture and your investors when the giants awaken. Will you sell your company to the big guys? Do you have a tactic to withstand their onslaught? Or do you plan to cash in early and be lounging by your Olympic-sized swimming pool before this happens? Whatever you expect, you need to cover this issue in your plan.

Maturing Industries

As industries mature, the rate of growth slows. This is happening today in the personal computer business and the Internet service provider (ISP) industry. It occurred recently in the video rental business and during the 1960s and 1970s in the automobile industry. Here is what typically happens in maturing industries:

Demand slows. While the industry may still be growing, the rate of demand for the products or services is beginning to diminish. This usually makes competition rougher, because the same number of businesses are fighting over fewer new customers.

Buyers become smarter. Customers become more sophisticated and demanding as they gain experience with new products or services. Perhaps when you bought your first VCR you didn't know enough to check if it could fast forward without turning the screen blank, but you certainly figured this out by the time you bought your next VCR. If your company is in a maturing industry, expect to see your customers quickly climb the learning curve and want to buy products with better features, or more options that deliver better value. This may make it harder to price your products high enough to be profitable.

Excess supply appears. As demand slows, it usually takes a while for manufacturers or suppliers to adjust their production. When supply exceeds demand, some suppliers cut prices to push their products out of inventory, which can reduce overall market prices and profit margins.

International competition increases. For manufactured products especially, foreign competitors who have lower labor costs or higher government subsidies can enter a market during this time and provide tough price competition. After a few years of DVD player sales, a low-cost Chinese manufacturer entered the U.S. market, underpricing the competition by nearly a third.

Profitability suffers. When competition spurs price cuts, profits suffer. Companies that are weak financially can fail or become takeover targets as soon as their profits decline.

Consolidation follows. When supply exceeds demand, profit margins diminish, and weaker companies face failure, a maturing industry usually enters a phase of consolidation in which bigger companies buy smaller companies, and some smaller companies combine to form larger ones.

The Best Strategies for Maturing Industries

Reduce cost. When profits are shrinking from lower prices, companies must strive to maintain profitability by reducing expenses. Ways of doing this include paying closer attention to efficiency, eliminating costly product features, or reducing the product line, so that the company can make fewer products more efficiently. Motorola dominated the cellular telephone industry during its early period, but when the industry began to mature and Motorola began to lose money, it cut back on its product line, eliminated features that consumers didn't seem to care about, and reduced its operating overhead.

Focus marketing on major customers. Steady customers with large orders can be serviced more efficiently than small customers who purchase in limited and sporadic quantities. It's also usually easier to maintain price competitiveness with the larger customers.

Expand to new markets. As existing markets become saturated and it becomes more difficult to remain profitable, you can expand to new markets with less competition and newer, less sophisticated customers.

Purchase rivals. One way to reduce competition is to purchase your competitors. When many small companies are bought up to form much bigger companies, it is sometimes referred to as a roll-up. This has happened among media businesses, accounting firms, hospitals, and car dealerships.

Think about well known, recently founded companies and see if their current strategies are a closer match to those companies on the list for maturing industries. As Jeff Bezos discusses in the Foreword, Amazon.com executed strategies for emerging industries when it opened for business—namely to get big fast and seize a strong market position. Since then, it has also worked to reduce its costs by focusing on efficiency, expanding its market to include more countries served and more types of products sold, and concentrating on service for bigger customers by using tactics such as free shipping for orders over $25. All of these strategies are effective in maturing industries, even if, in this case, the industry is only a few years old.

Stagnant and Declining Industries

Industries shrinking or experiencing zero growth are called stagnant or declining industries. The mattress and pillow industries were stagnant for many years until innovative products, such as allergy-proof bedding, and new marketing techniques, such as catalog sales, revitalized them. The candle industry suffered decades of decline until the 1990s, when significant numbers of successful, upscale candle stores were established.

The Best Strategies for Stagnant or Declining Industries

Focus on niches, especially growing niches. In addition to allergy-proof products, the bed and pillow industries have focused on people with back and neck problems, a growing group as the American population has aged and grown heavier. They also target their advertising to magazines, newspapers, and television shows that reach wealthier, older audiences.

Differentiate and innovate. The candle industry has innovated by creating new designs, such as long-lasting candles, and by adding various aromas, as well as encouraging entrepreneurs to open candle boutiques.

Reduce cost wherever possible. Cost reduction is always a good strategy, because it allows a company to stay profitable even if it needs to cut prices. In the bedding industry, for example, companies started selling directly to consumers through direct mail catalogs, in addition to supplying their retailers. This reduced costs, and allowed them to target consumers who were too busy to shop in stores and wanted fast delivery of bulky items.

Fragmented Industries

Industries with many competitors, none of which has a large market share, are called fragmented industries. They include businesses such as restaurants, lawn-care companies, building contractors, and florists. Fragmented industries are generally easy to enter, because they require only low levels of investment, which accounts for the constant stream of new competitors in these businesses. It's also difficult for fragmented businesses to remain efficient as they grow.

A non-fragmented company, such as General Motors, can make a million cars per year with a lower cost per car than if it made only 1,000 cars annually. However, restaurants, plumbers, florists, and other fragmented industry enterprises, can't benefit from these efficiencies, called *economies of scale*, as they grow. In fact, it can even become more expensive to provide their products or services as they grow.

For example, if a pizzeria owner wants to open an additional restaurant in another neighborhood, he may save a little money on bulk food purchases, but he must hire the same number of waitresses per customer and cooks per meal in order to maintain the excellent service he offers his clientele in the original location. He will also be forced to hire a full-time manager at the new restaurant, since he won't be able to be in two places at the same time. Because of such issues, businesses in fragmented industries tend to focus primarily on local markets.

The Best Strategies for Fragmented Industries

Focus on the local market. Because of the characteristics of these fragmented industries, one rarely sees regional plumbing companies or regional florists. The successful ones are those that focus on building clientele in their local markets.

Specialize your product or service. As businesses in fragmented markets specialize, they can gain a competitive advantage, maintain strong prices, and become profitable. Bakeries that concentrate on elaborate wedding cakes, health clubs that offer personal trainers, or lawn-care companies that specialize in sports fields, are all examples of this strategy.

Create formula facilities. In order to expand, businesses in fragmented industries need to create simple, standardized, no-frills, formula facilities. Examples of companies employing this strategy include FedEx Kinko's, McDonald's, Bally's Total Fitness, and Subway sandwich stores. Formula facilities also open the door to franchising.

Keep costs down. Fragmented markets are, by definition, very competitive. Only businesses that control their costs can withstand the constant onslaught of new competitors who try to gain a foothold by underpricing the competition.

Industries with Dominant Leaders

Successful industry leaders such as Microsoft, Toyota, or McDonald's, stay on the offensive by constantly striving to improve their operations and efficiency, and by bringing out new, more popular products. They continually promote and advertise to fortify their brands, and only reduce prices as a last resort to maintain their market share. When they do it right, as these three companies have, they are tough competitors.

Not all dominant leaders do it right. Before being purchased by SBC Communications in 2005, AT&T had withered to a shadow of the untouchable giant it once was. It lost its technology edge when management concentrated on stock price through short-term strategies, such as selling divisions, and through regulatory changes that opened the door to new competitors. Kmart, the successor to the venerable Kresge Department store company, filed for bankruptcy in 2002 because its older, smaller stores and weaker management couldn't keep up with competition from Wal-Mart, Target, Kohls', and others.

This means that you can develop a business strategy to battle the big guys and win.

The Best Strategies for Competing with Dominant Leaders

Focus on the long term. Large companies tend to focus on their quarterly financial performance, because this is how Wall Street evaluates them. They can miss the long-term trends or be reluctant to invest in long-term projects. The music industry refused to understand the impact of digital recordings until Internet-based services, such as Napster, began to hurt them significantly. Now, traditional music companies are buying digital services to catch up.

Take risks. Corporate managers are...corporate. They can be rather bureaucratic and reluctant to take risks that might endanger that next big bonus, or a long-awaited promotion. New York Mayor Michael Bloomberg made himself a billionaire by playing the role of David and taking on the Goliaths in the financial-information industry, mainly large banks and brokerage houses. He took a risk and built a better system and now his system has come to dominate much of this industry.

Know the market. Corporate managers tend to believe that they know the market better than their customers do. In what is probably the worst business decision of all time, Western Union turned down purchasing Alexander Graham Bell's telephone because they didn't think enough people would want it. Pursue your judgment of what will sell. If the big guys don't see it, think of Alexander Graham Bell.

These weaknesses among big companies create what has been rightfully called the *attacker's advantage*. So, if you're a David and want to confront a Goliath, don't despair. With an attacker's advantage based on a long-term focus, your knowledge of the market and your willingness to take risks, you can still compete with the big guys.

It is important to match the strategies you use to reach your business goals to the characteristics of your specific industry. Be

﹂ sure your strategies are outwardly focused and geared to your best competitive advantage. Make certain that they will impress potential investors and lenders as being the most powerful means to achieve your business goals—and theirs.

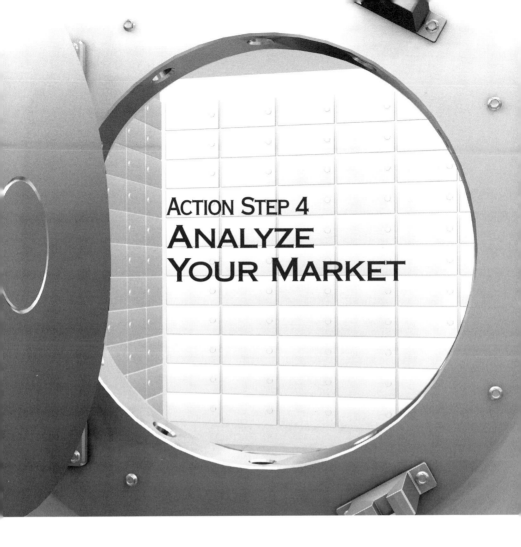

ACTION STEP 4
ANALYZE YOUR MARKET

WHO WILL WANT YOUR PRODUCT OR SERVICE?

Identifying your market is one of the great satisfactions of starting your own business. You're imagining actual people using your product or service, and how they will be as pleased buying it as you are selling it.

To determine your targeted market, write down the demographics of the people who will use your product or service. How old are they? What do they do for a living? Will mostly women use your service? Is your product or service attractive to a particular ethnic or economic group? Will only the wealthy be able to afford it? Does your ideal customer live in a certain type of neighborhood, such as a suburb, in order to use your lawn mower? Answering these questions about the demographics of your prime market will help you establish the clear characteristics of the people you need to reach.

If you're selling soap, you may believe that every dirty body needs your product, but you can't start with the entire world as your initial market. Even if you've developed such a ubiquitous item as soap, you need to identify a smaller, more targeted customer group first, such as children under eight, for the bubble gum-scented bubble bath. If your soap only works with pumped well water without fluoride, you must acknowledge that your intended market has geographical limits as well.

If the major benefit of your soap is that it doesn't cause eyes to tear upon contact, your primary customers will probably be children under age eight or, rather, their parents, who do the actual shopping. If your soap contains pumice that will remove car grease, paint, and tile cement without toxic chemicals or fumes, your market will be defined by people who work at specific professions, say, mechanics, house painters, and bathroom contractors. It may be that your product works well on removing garden dirt, too, or that many grownups don't like to cry when they get soap in their eyes, but you want to make sure that you have targeted the best buyers first. The more focused your market, the more convincing your plan will be. You can always branch out later.

Establishing the size of your potential market is important, too. This will be easier once you've completed the demographic analysis. Then you'll be able to research the numbers: how many car mechanics, house painters or bathroom contractors are there in any given community? How many children in the United States are currently under the age of eight? How much soap will they use in a month or a year? How many other soap manufacturers already have a share of the market? How big are your potential competitors? Do any of them make bubble gum-scented soap? And, where do you find the answers to all of these questions?

There are three aspects of a marketing plan that fall under the heading "more is better." These are research, targeting, and testing. The more of each you do and provide to your potential funders, the better and more convincing your plan will be—and the more likely your business will succeed.

Your marketing strategy begins with a carefully researched, highly specific description of your target market. If you're building welding tools for use in manufacturing and modifying cars, you need to research potential customers and the competitive products they currently use. Based on this, you will be able to create a list of the companies that need your product, as well as the names of the people at each company who make the purchasing decisions. Finally, you can actually test for market acceptance of your product by speaking with people in the industry.

If you're selling poles for pole vaulters, you can research the colleges and universities that train pole vaulters and the coaches who decide which poles to buy. From this information, you can create a list of potential customers, and test your concept by speaking with coaches and athletes.

If you're opening a clothing store for teenage girls, you should research this market by collecting industry and consumption pattern data, and by researching the stores that currently sell in the geographic areas you are considering. Based on this research, you will be able to define your potential market by demographic characteristics such as age, geography, income, and race. Finally, you can test your concept by interviewing teenage girls who are in your target group, and actually asking them if they would shop at the kind of store you envision.

The three most important guidelines to follow in defining your target market are:

1. Research your potential market thoroughly
2. Target your market like a bull's-eye
3. Test before you launch

1. Research Your Potential Market Thoroughly

Whether your business plan specifies six potential customers or millions, you must learn a great deal about them. The end of the book lists some helpful resources for consumer data, if you're targeting a broad consumer market. You can also commission or carry out your own research to test consumer reaction to your concept by phone surveys, in-person interviews, or consumer focus groups. This can be very expensive if you hire a professional research company, so try to invest some of your own time in speaking directly with members of your target group.

Identifying and defining your target market in the following ways will help you create the most convincing marketing campaign possible:

- **By geography**, so you can locate your business near specific markets or target your advertising to reach potential customers most efficiently.

- **By demographics**, so you will understand such customer characteristics as age, gender, and ethnicity in tailoring your advertising messages and focusing your marketing efforts.

- **By season**, so you can schedule your marketing efforts when buying is most likely.

- **By purchasing patterns**, so you can identify products or services that tend to be bought at the same time, and match your marketing to those trends.

Understanding your competition and their strategies is key to positioning and promoting your product or service. For each competitor you can:

Collect their printed promotional materials.

Record their broadcast advertising to analyze their messages and determine their marketing expenditures.

Develop a profile of their customers based on industry research, interviews with experts, or by simply watching and recording the characteristics of people who enter their stores.

Create a comprehensive view of their product line, including each product's characteristics and price.

Prepare a corporate history that details each competitor's business development, including various marketing strategies.

Understanding the history of your industry will help you to see the big trends. For example, the food industry has experienced major changes with the increase of two-income households. With both men and women in the workforce, the demand for traditional food products that require lots of preparation has decreased, while the craving for prepared foods that can be put on the table quickly has increased.

The gradual graying of our population has affected the health club industry by increasing the demand for low impact exercise equipment that works the cardiovascular system but is gentle on aging joints. Seeing the history and trends in your industry will help you position and market your business effectively.

Similarly, gathering financial information such as pricing, profit margins, bank lending practices, and investor interest will be enormously useful in building your financial projections. Much of this information can be obtained from bankers, investors, and industry experts.

In my experience, most people will make themselves available and talk candidly with prospective business owners in their industry. Also, as I discuss in Action Step 10, a great deal of this information can be obtained in a library or from the Risk Management Association.

Your Field Trip to the Library

Plan on spending at least one entire day in a library, preferably a business library. I have spent thousands of hours in libraries and, although electronic databases have revolutionized the process and speed of research, taking the time to read through material carefully is still the best way to unearth useful information, whether it's on a computer screen, on microfilm, or in a dusty old bound journal.

In the Resources at the back, I list the databases that I find extremely useful, but the specifics of your industry will largely determine which ones are best for your research. Look at industry-oriented magazines, newsletters, journals, and databases. Use the *Readers' Guide to Periodical Literature* to research products or industries in general business publications. *The Wall Street Journal, Forbes,* and *BusinessWeek* cover almost every industry, often profiling specific businesses and interviewing CEOs of both large and fledgling corporations.

Academic journals may not be particularly entertaining to read, but they cover a vast array of subjects. Sometimes an academic journal will publish a study that uses a sample of businesses in your industry to analyze a subject of scholarly interest. Read it, because it may provide statistics and marketing information which will make your business plan even more persuasive and bankable.

Don't forget to talk to the librarians. Most hold advanced degrees in library science, and all are familiar with the tools and organization of their particular facilities. They're experts and are there to help you reduce wasteful research time. Tap their brains and knowledge. They'll be honored and you will be rewarded.

Business Resource Centers

Small Business Development Centers (SBDCs) are local outreach offices of the federal Small Business Administration (SBA). They house useful information about their local markets, data on virtually every industry, and sample business plans. Many state and local governments have business resource centers to encourage economic development in their regions. Staff members are often very knowledgeable about data sources on the local economy and business environment.

The Web—a Useful Resource, but Caveat Emptor

The good news is that there is a huge amount of information available on the web. The bad news is that you cannot make the web the cornerstone of your research efforts. Many websites exist to generate sales for products, to disseminate information to influence government policy, to sell memberships, or to publicize someone. Sometimes websites sell government data that you can obtain free (as they did).

In addition, the sources of the data are often not stated and even if they are, an independent website may not be playing by the same rules as established, well-respected data sources that you can find in the library. It is often hard to tell the good websites from those that are best avoided because their agendas can interfere with the objectivity and accuracy of their information. If you ask yourself what is the website's agenda, you may come to the conclusion that using its data or opinions as part of the foundation of your business could be a big mistake.

In the Resources, I list the sites I find most useful, including the SBA and census sites. Industry associations may also have useful sites. Beyond that, you are venturing into dangerous web waters.

Research Relevant Regulation

Every business must function in an environment of government regulation. Think about it: taxes, employee benefits, construction codes, and contracts—just to name a few areas—are all tightly controlled by regulation. Identifying the key regulatory restrictions that will make an impact on your venture is one of the major tasks in analyzing the market for your proposed business.

If you're opening a restaurant, you will probably need an operating license, and your employees may have to complete mandated training in food handling. There are probably regulations controlling noise levels, food delivery times, garbage pickup rules and greasy kitchen exhaust limits, as well as special licensing fees and taxes to pay, all of which must be included in your proposed budget.

Any business that requires construction will have to cope with zoning regulations, obtaining a certificate of occupancy and complying with literally hundreds of individual building codes. Although your architect or contractor will be able to handle the specific details, your business plan must address these concerns to make certain that regulations and zoning rules will not interfere with your building design, parking lot size or operating hours. Upcoming changes in regulations could affect your product or service, so you will need to speak with government officials, lawyers, politicians, and other business owners.

I know of a restaurant in the Midwest that planned to open on a main road leading into town. The owner didn't check with local officials and, a few weeks after opening his diner, the town changed the traffic patterns and the number of cars passing the restaurant dropped by more than 60 percent. Three months later, the restaurant closed. If the entrepreneur had met with local officials or had attended local town council meetings, this disaster could have been avoided.

Many, perhaps most, regulations, are actually good for business. For example, tough licensing standards limit competition. Government granted franchises, such as those for cable television, broadcast stations, taxicabs, or even hot dog stands, often amount to government-protected monopolies. In many industries, such as education, health, and transportation, mandated government expenditures are the main source of income. Make sure your business plan delineates the way government regulations affect your business—both positively and negatively.

Target Your Market Like A Bull's-Eye

The more tightly defined your target market, the more likely your plan will attract funding sources. Accurately identifying prospective purchasers of your product or service will produce the greatest return on your marketing expenditures.

Suppose your business is Howie's House of Hubcaps, specializing in replacement hubcaps for 1955 to 1960 Chevys. On one hand, you could advertise during the Superbowl, but that would bankrupt you and waste the vast majority of your advertising budget to reach people who don't own 1955 to 1960 Chevys. On the other hand, if your research revealed vintage Chevy clubs that sell ads in their newsletters or would sell you their lists, restorers who specialize in these cars, or annual gatherings of owners of vintage Chevys, you could build an effective marketing program very cheaply. This would make the financials look better and impress your potential investors.

If your plan is to open Bobbie's Sox, a store selling a wide variety of socks, your research might give you information about the age, income, professions, and gender of people who tend to spend the most money on socks. Then you can target your location, store design, inventory choices, and advertising to this segment of the market that purchases the most socks.

Understanding the motivations of your potential customers will help you target customer groups for your marketing strategy. Examples of customer motivation include:

- Low price
- Status
- Quality
- Speed of delivery
- Service
- Design

For example, if you have a glassware manufacturing business, you need to find out what influences your customers. Do they tend to buy your product when they purchase a second home, or rent a new apartment following a divorce? Is it an item that young couples list on their wedding registries? Or do customers view your glassware as a basic product they buy any time because of function, design, and price? Answers to these questions can help you identify the appropriate target market and incorporate its description into your plan. An executive for IKEA told me that two of their best markets consisted of people buying country homes outside big cities, and people getting divorced who need to set up new homes fast. This knowledge helped IKEA to organize its stores, price its products, and plan one of its most memorable and successful promotions: "starting up or starting over."

A Chinese student of mine was sought out by parents in her Brooklyn neighborhood who were raising adopted babies from China. They wanted her advice about how to keep their children connected to their Chinese heritage. She thought there might be a business selling Chinese children's books, language lessons, clothing, and other products to this highly targeted market. Within a short time, she had researched the size and characteristics of the market, talked to many parents in her neighborhood, and communicated with friends in China to estimate the costs of purchasing products for children. Her business became profitable within a few months, which is more than most dot.com business founders can say. Today *www.chinasprout.com* continues to thrive by applying strategies that helped it grow from the initial 100 products sold to its small, original market, to providing over 3,000 products to a much broader market, including retailers, educators and wholesalers.

Test Before You Launch

You will increase the effectiveness of your marketing strategy if you actually test your concepts first. A successful test will also greatly increase the confidence potential investors will have in your plan. This test could take the form of a small mailing to prospective customers asking them if they would order your product once it's available, or making sales calls on prospective customers and seeing their reactions.

Remember that your plan must convince readers of the efficacy of your idea. There is a Harvard Business School case study on the startup of *Parenting* magazine, which shows the plan that the founder of the business, Robin Wolaner, used to attract investors. The plan is thorough and sensible, but the most convincing part is the results of the test mailing to young parents asking them to subscribe. These results clearly showed that a larger mailing would attract enough subscribers to make the magazine successful, which is exactly what happened. In the *Parenting* magazine case, the mailing was itself a significant expenditure. If your budget doesn't allow for that, there are still many alternatives:

- **Arrange to put sample products** in stores to see how they sell.

- **Make sales calls on prospective clients or customers**, and ask them if they will commit to buying as soon as your business is up and running.

- **Interview potential customers** and industry experts to solicit their opinions of your business idea.

- **Study the performance** of close competitors. This can include counting the foot traffic into their stores, estimating their revenue from public databases such as Dun and Bradstreet, or from private sources such as lawyers, accountants, or past employees.

- **Run your own research program** with focus groups, consisting of approximately a dozen consumers in your target group, at which you discuss your proposed products or services.

- **Talk to customers** of a business you are planning to buy to find out how satisfied they are with the products or services they currently receive, and what ideas they have for improvements.

Careful testing will give you useful information about how the market will view your product or service, and it will add considerable credibility to your plan.

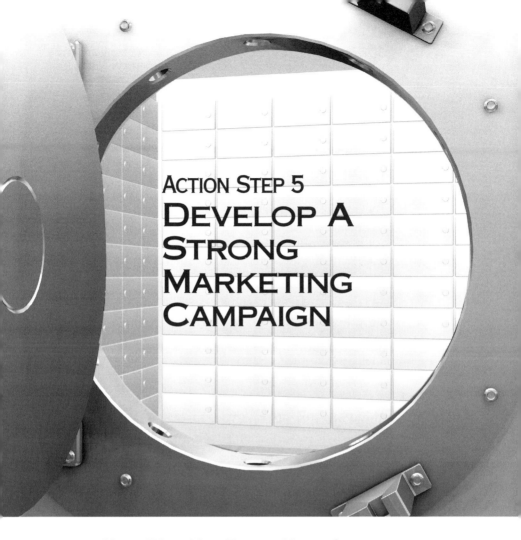

Action Step 5
Develop A Strong Marketing Campaign

How Will You Reach Your Customers And What Will You Say To Them?

Entrepreneurs, especially inventors, often believe that their business concepts are so spectacular that promoting their product or service won't be necessary—sort of a build-it-and-they-will-come attitude, especially if what you're building is the proverbial better mousetrap. One of the most common flaws I see in plans is the entrepreneur's failure to describe exactly how customers will be reached and how products will be presented to them. Potential investors, staff, and partners won't be convinced that your idea can succeed until you've established well-researched and effective methods of contacting your customers—and the assurance that once you've reached them, you can convince them to buy your product or service. After you have defined, researched, and tested your market as much as you can, you need to develop a plan to reach your potential customers.

Marketing describes how you will position and let your potential customers know about your product or service. *Positioning* means concentrating on the competitive advantages you have identified: will your product or service distinguish itself by its superior quality, its revolutionary features, or its ability to make your customers happier than they've ever been in their lives? Marketing also establishes the best ways to reach your potential customers and precisely what you should say to them.

Suppose you're a hypothetical Field Center client who wants to open a financial services business to advise Wall Street investors who wish to buy stocks in the rubber sole industry. You've already identified your competitive advantage as your unparalleled expertise in these investments, and your target market as major New York City-based investors interested in rubber sole stocks.

Some of the questions you'll have to ask yourself before you develop a marketing campaign include: what trade journals and newspapers do your potential clients read? Would ads in these publications be worth the cost of placing them? Which websites are frequently visited by your potential customers? How could you interest a reporter for one of these periodicals in writing a story about your new advisory firm? Is there an organization of rubber sole company investors that you should join? Are there conventions for investors in rubber sole companies that would be worth attending? Will your knowledge of a related industry, such as flip flop manufacturing, give you more impressive credentials in finding clients? Will direct mailings to investors or posting information on the Internet be useful outlets?

When you have the right marketing campaign in place, you have an operating plan to gain market share, generate revenue, and bring your financial projections into reality.

I remember three clients coming to the Field Center with various baked goods they wished to market: brownies, scones and cupcakes. All of their products were delicious—I know, I tasted them—but the brownie baker opened his store next to a McDonald's, so the existing foot traffic was all wrong for $3.00 chocolate squares. The superb scone maker tried to bake and package and market all on her own—and ended up burning herself out.

The only client who succeeded was the cupcake guy, who plotted his course thoroughly by finding the right spot (an albeit expensive booth in the city's recently refurbished train station), the right price (people didn't think twice about buying a cupcake for $2.00, and came back for more) and the right promotion (he hired a college student part time to hand out samples during the morning and evening rush hours). Within a month, he was clearing enough profit to drop the samples and hire full-time counter help.

The difference between the successful cupcake guy, and the brownie baker and the scone maker, was a well-developed marketing plan. There are some highly successful companies that were founded on little more than a solid marketing plan. Nike, the shoe and athletic-wear giant, owns no factories and operates very few retail stores. Nike contracts with existing factories around the world to make its products and ship them directly to retailers, such as WalMart or Macy's. Nike owns a few warehouses, but that's it. Instead of owning supermarkets for shoes, Nike is a super marketer of shoes. Nike creates the brands, markets the products to potential customers to create demand, and arranges for distribution to retailers.

I have often thought of real estate companies such as Century 21 in the same way. They neither build nor own houses. They are contract marketers for people who own houses and want to sell them. In fact, most retailers are basically marketing organizations. They manufacture little or nothing of what they sell. The key to their success is finding a good location, creating an attractive atmosphere, choosing the right mix of products to sell, pricing their products competitively, and delivering excellent service. These are all marketing functions.

The Four Ps

All marketing campaigns are based on The Four Ps:

The **Product** or service.
The **Price** you will charge.
The **Place** you will sell or distribute your goods or service.
The **Promotion** and advertising you will use to communicate with potential customers.

Product

Your business plan must make a compelling case for why customers will want to purchase your product or service. After analyzing thousands of business plans, I have identified the most persuasive reasons:

Convenience. Domino's Pizza is built entirely on making it easier and faster to eat pizza through a superior delivery service.

New products. It's rare that a totally new product emerges, but you could be one of the few to do it, like Alexander Graham Bell and his telephone. More recent examples are e-mail, wireless messaging devices, and DVD players.

New applications. Many people have built successful businesses by finding one more function for a computer during those idle hours when it just sits on someone's desk. Video games, calendar functions, and spreadsheet programs can all be considered new applications for an existing product. The Sony Walkman was developed as a pocket memo and dictation machine for businesspeople, but found a much bigger application and audience by playing music.

Improved performance. A product may be more attractive to customers by being noisier (motorcycle engines), quieter (dishwasher motors), smelling better (deodorant), or not smelling at all (deodorant). Successful marketing is based on improving the performance of a product in the minds of consumers.

Status. Rolex, Jaguar, Dom Perignon, Versace, and Sub-Zero products are all marketed, at least in part, on their status appeal. People buy these items hoping that they will not only run well or taste good, but that their prestige will rub off on the purchaser.

Packaging. A product's container draws attention on the shelf and sends a message to consumers. Big packages, such as jumbo plastic laundry detergent jugs, shout *value.* Small packages, such as concentrated laundry detergent in recyclable cardboard boxes, say *convenience* and *environmental responsibility.* Pharmaceutical companies repackage medications in extra-strength formulas, which are really just two pills squeezed into one, creating new life for old products.

Appearance and styling. The automobile industry has thrived for decades on minor styling changes to create demand for new cars. Flashy fins in the 1960s didn't improve the function of the car—just the appearance. Or at least they made last year's models look dated. Now that computers are commonplace, styling is playing a more important role. Does a see-through computer casing turn you on? Is gel toothpaste a new product or just a styling change?

Remember that you don't need to have a revolutionary product to have a successful business. In fact, it may be quite the contrary. Entrepreneurs with revolutionary business ideas often have trouble recruiting the resources they need. Alexander Graham Bell had a hard time convincing people to invest in his newfangled device, the telephone. Then he had a great deal of difficulty getting businesses and individuals to adopt it.

Sometimes the most compelling business idea is one that takes a widely used and accepted product and just changes it.

John D. Rockefeller didn't invent oil; he set up a system to control its manufacturing and distribution. Tom Monaghan, the founder of Domino's, didn't invent pizza; he developed a system that delivers pizza faster.

Price

Deciding on a price for your product is key to any bankable business plan. Most of us assume that lower prices are better because we're so conditioned as consumers to look for bargains. Price is an issue that investors, bankers, and partners will carefully scrutinize. However, look before you leap down to a low price for your product because:

- It's more difficult to raise prices than to lower them.
- Low prices sometimes send a message of low *quality*.
- You need to make a profit.

If you charge too little for your product and can't make a profit, you may not be able to raise prices quickly enough to save your business. Your business plan won't be bankable if you can't turn a profit. Your plan has to demonstrate that you can sell enough widgets at a profit-generating price—not just at a price that will make customers flock to you.

Sometimes companies focus on low price too much. If you have a low-cost means of manufacturing a product that is difficult for others to copy, or you have a patent, copyright, or license that protects your product, your competition may not be able to match your price. In fact, if you focus more on price than your customers, charging a low price may hurt your profitability without actually providing a major competitive advantage.

Several new discount airlines focused on price as a key element of their strategy until their larger and better-financed competitors took notice and reduced their prices even further, making the upstarts lose customers or lose money on every ticket. Most discount airlines didn't last long. They should have focused on something other than just price. While JetBlue has had a major focus on price, it has also given great attention to service and comfort as competitive advantages.

Place

If you are opening a store, never forget the rule of "location, location, location." Sometimes a great location—which puts your business right where your customers are—will overcome virtually any weakness. I remember stopping at a gas station at the edge of a desert. This was literally the last gas station for a few hundred miles. The gas was 50% more expensive than gas anywhere else in the state, the owner was unfriendly, the service was rude, and the station only accepted payment in cash. None of this made for a happy customer experience, but it probably didn't hurt sales either, because this gas station had the right location!

Place, which also includes how you will manage distribution, is, in my experience, the most overlooked element of many marketing plans. A publishing industry consultant once said to me "publishing is fundamentally a distribution business." I was shocked. What about great books, glowing reviews, beautiful stores, and word-of-mouth? Well, those are all important, but it means little if there aren't enough books in the stores, or they can't be found by customers, or there are too few bookstores. If too few books are distributed, potential buyers leave stores empty-handed. Bookstores lose money when too many books are distributed and they end up on the remainder table. So much for great books!

To avoid these pitfalls, I urge you to answer the following questions:

• How will the purchaser obtain your product?

• How do your competitors distribute? Do they use wholesalers or distributors as middlemen?

- Have your competitors locked up all the established distribution channels, making it hard for you to reach your customers?

- How will you manage distribution so that you know where your products are and what areas are experiencing shortages?

- How will you focus your distribution? On the most likely markets, within a certain geographic area, or where your competition is weak?

- Is there an alternative distribution channel available, such as discount retailers, direct-to-consumer advertising or the Internet that could give you an advantage? The gateway to the Internet, and the countless millions of prospective customers for your product or service, is your company's website.

Your Website

Just about every business needs a website, and your website should be an integral part of your plan. Your investors, partners, lenders and anyone else who reads your plan will want to know that you will take full advantage of the opportunities afforded by the Internet. There are a vast number of options for your venture's website. The costs vary just as widely. Your plan for your website should include these elements:

The website's purpose. Your website can be informational to communicate your business's location, the services you provide, or its history. The site might also be designed to service existing customers by allowing them to make appointments or check their accounts. The site could be a virtual store which handles selling functions directly. Alternatively, the site might be intended to convert prospects into customers by promoting your business and encouraging them to call or visit your physical location.

A commitment for a professional design. People will judge you and your business based on your website, so it must look professional and make a strong first impression. Websites are great tools for new and growing businesses because even small businesses can look big on the Internet. But that also places a burden on you to have a site that is just as professional, credible, and well-functioning as your competitors. Creating that website requires a team that includes a designer, who lays out the site for function and gives it a visual style, and a programmer who will convert the design into computer code. Stating your intention to create a strong site and identifying who will be the members of your online team should be part of your bankable business plan.

A system for tracking. Every click on a website by every visitor is recorded and tallied. This provides a great trove of information that you can use to measure the performance of your site, see how visitors are navigating the site, and help you to improve it. Your home page functions are your store window and the better they are, the more people will enter this virtual store to explore, learn, and buy. The company that hosts your site can track all these patterns and allow you to access this data whenever you want. Your bankable business plan should discuss specifically how you will access the information about your site's performance and how committed you are to continuously updating and improving your site.

A plan for marketing your site. There are literally billions of websites so your bankable business plan needs to include a marketing plan for "driving traffic" to your site. People find websites through search engines such as Google and Yahoo!, by bookmarking them from previous visits, from links at other sites, and by learning about them from advertising. Putting your website's address on all your printed materials and on all retail store signs as well as mentioning it on radio and television ads, and negotiating links from other sites will greatly improve the effectiveness of your site.

E-mail campaigns. Building a list of the e-mail addresses of your existing and potential customers opens up the door to marketing via e-mail. While people detest uninvited e-mail or spam, e-mail from businesses they have invited or approved is highly effective and inexpensive. Your marketing plan will greatly benefit from specific ideas for using e-mail as a tool. As with your website, you will be able to track what percentage of people open your e-mail, how many click through to your site from your e-mail, and how many of those actually make a purchase.

Promotion

Promotion is how your potential customers find out about your product or service. You might place advertisements in trade magazines, drum up news coverage, convince retail stores to display your product, develop a direct-mail solicitation, rely on word-of-mouth from satisfied customers, or any of a dozen other ways to create awareness of, and demand for, your product.

Coupons, free samples, free trial periods, volume purchase incentives, in-store displays, manufacturer's rebates, financial incentives to distributors, contests, and premiums are all examples of sales promotions. AOL has distributed millions of CDs that give new customers thousands of free hours if they just try AOL. Airline bonus miles and coupons for products sold in supermarkets have become standard in their respective industries.

Before I review each method of reaching your customers, consider these points in creating an effective promotion plan:

Be specific. Your promotion plan must be precise and detailed. If you intend to use coupons to publicize your product or service, you must explain the terms of the coupon, decide on how it will be distributed, and determine how many coupons you expect to get back.

State your goals. Explain what you expect to accomplish and why you are using this means of promotion. Having a product booth at a convention attended by many of your customers is a clear, focused way to reach your market. Many companies that have booths at conventions put on special promotions just for purchases made at the convention to encourage customers to buy before the convention ends.

Establish a system of measurement. If you expect your newspaper ads to bring people into your clothing store, then you need a way of measuring traffic—before, during, and after the ads appear in the paper. With coupons, you need a way to track how many have been distributed and how many are being redeemed. Tracking results can be complex but quite possible with Internet advertising and promotion. It is easy to tally how many people visit a website or click through to an ad or another page as well as the number of people who actually make a purchase or contact you.

Hold your expenses accountable. All of your promotional and marketing efforts will have costs in the form of time and money expended. Like any other expenses, such as manufacturing materials or labor, marketing costs should be held accountable for the benefit they produce.

Suppose your promotional plan for your tuba factory calls for sponsoring concerts of a 100-member tuba orchestra playing Christmas Carols at holiday events throughout your city. This will involve a great deal of staff time and some specific expenditures, such as hiring a bus to transport the orchestra members and all those bulky tubas. Maybe you'll need to rent three buses. If you are hoping that this promotion will increase tuba sales, then you should set a specific goal and establish a system of measurement.

If your typical sales in the first quarter of each year in your city equal ten tubas, perhaps you are hoping that you will sell twenty tubas in the first quarter following the tuba orchestra promotional events in December. Track your sales, measure them, and set up a system whereby staff can ask tuba purchasers what inspired them to buy a tuba. You might want to distribute flyers with a discount coupon at each of the performances, which purchasers will then have to bring to your factory store in order to receive the discount.

With this information, you can decide if the tuba events increased actual sales and if the expense and effort were worthwhile. If they were, you might want to consider making the tuba orchestra an ongoing event every December and maybe add a Labor Day weekend concert in your city's band shell for the fall. Demonstrating in your business plan that you will hold all of your expenditures accountable, even marketing and promotional events, will greatly impress your plan's readers.

There are two basic methods of reaching your customers: through *paid advertising* or *free media*. Let's take a look at these approaches so you understand their respective benefits and drawbacks.

Paid Advertising

Television, billboards, radio, newspapers, website ads, magazines, and even blimps comprise some of the many options for paid advertising and represent a major element of promotion. A great advantage of paid advertising is that it can deliver highly quantified measurements of how many people will see or hear your ad, since professionals who sell space and time slots keep very detailed records of their effectiveness.

Paid advertising is measured in *reach*, the number of different people who will see or hear your ad, and by *frequency*, the average number of times each of those people will see or hear your ad. Reach multiplied by frequency gives you the total number of *impressions* your advertising will make.

In my experience, frequency is more important than reach. We are all exposed to dozens or even hundreds of ads daily. Most go in one ear and out the other! The key is to deliver the same message to the same people multiple times to ensure that your message is received.

To plan your advertising campaign, follow these steps:

Research how your competitors advertise. You have probably already noticed every competitor's ad—much more so than their customers have! Create a table in your plan that lists every competitor, where they advertise, and the message their ads convey, such as price, sales, or special features.

Talk with advertising representatives. Advertising salespeople from radio stations, magazines, and other media outlets are a great source of information about how your competitors are advertising and what your options are. Meet with them, tell them you're developing a media plan, ask about your competitors' advertising campaigns, and see what they suggest. Most will give you specific information about your competitors and good suggestions about how you can develop your own advertising strategy effectively.

Develop a focused and accountable plan. Take all this information and distill it into the best method of reaching your most important target markets. Your plan should include the reach and frequency data that the advertising representatives give you, as well as detailed cost estimates. Describe what you expect to achieve in terms of foot traffic into your store, or calls from potential customers, or name recognition within target markets. Finally, develop your system for tracking results and holding these expenditures accountable.

Free Media

Business owners love the idea of attracting all kinds of attention to their products or services without having to spend a penny.
A good example of this occurred in 2002 when inventor Dean Kamen unveiled his riding device, Segway, The Human Transporter.
It attracted huge amounts of attention on the evening news and in
newspapers. Companies, such as Amazon.com and Yahoo!, were
competing to give one away in exchange for publicizing it. Let me
clue you in on one major fact: free media *ain't* free.

It's not that NBC was paid to put the story on the evening
news. It's that an enormous amount of thought, effort, time,
and expense went into creating this story. For years, Kamen's
company had been building interest in its upcoming product
by spreading the word that he was working on a revolutionary invention. Keeping it a mystery helped raise interest and
expectations, so hype was built far in advance of the product's
unveiling.

When the Segway was finally revealed, the company had
already produced professional-quality video clips, still photo-
graphs, and news releases. Its paid staff members contacted
the media and arranged for interviews, demonstrations, and
test drives. And, of course, millions were spent to produce
this innovative machine. The company continues to generate
free media coverage by alerting local newspapers and television
stations whenever a city buys Segways for their police force or
a major business purchases them for navigating their gigantic
warehouses, but this, too, is the result of the efforts of paid professional promoters.

Free media is great, but it takes a huge amount of planning,
expense, and effort, and it carries no guarantee of success. If you
schedule a grand opening for your new store and your city is hit
by a record snowfall, I can assure you, no one will hear of your
store, regardless of the blockbuster events you had arranged.

Here are some guidelines for developing the free media element of your bankable business plan:

Write up specific story concepts you think could attract attention. Maybe you are a former IBM executive who's starting a software company, or you're a retired but beloved ballerina who's opening a dance school. Perhaps your recycling business will be the first to use a new technology. Write the stories and put them in an appendix to your business plan.

Make certain that the stories enhance your business plan. I once read a story about a former convict who started a security business. Did he actually think that this would bring him customers? Or entice investors?

Plan for the long term. You can't control whether the media will take to your idea, when they will use it, or how much attention they will give it. Most successful free media efforts put out a steady stream of potential stories. Some get picked up, others don't. Persistence can pay off—eventually. Stating this specifically in your plan and outlining your free media approaches will impress potential investors and lenders.

Every bankable business plan must include an effective marketing strategy in which you describe how you will reach your customers and what you will say to them. As you design your marketing campaign, keep the Four Ps uppermost in your mind: product, price, place, and promotion. This is the portion of the business plan that convinces lenders and investors that you will be able to gain market share, generate revenue, and bring your financial projections to fruition.

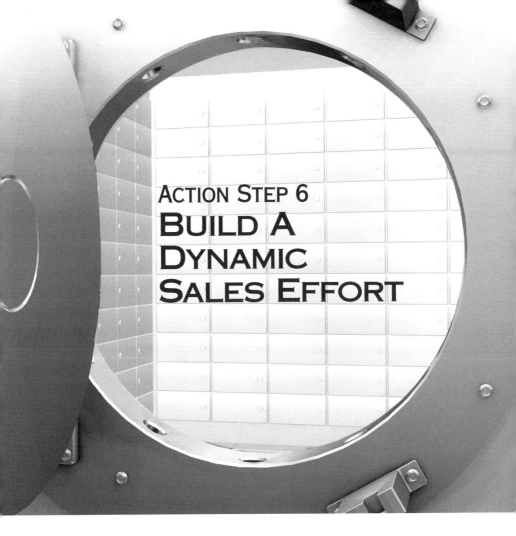

ACTION STEP 6
BUILD A DYNAMIC SALES EFFORT

HOW WILL YOU ATTRACT CUSTOMERS?

Potential investors and bankers want to know that you are highly sales oriented. They have all seen entrepreneurs with great ideas go down in flames because they didn't build a strong sales effort.

First, you should be clear about how sales is different from marketing. *Marketing* is the overall way in which you position and promote your product or service. It covers areas such as advertising, market research, distribution, and packaging. *Sales* is the interaction with your customers that produces orders. Sales is the specific process that takes place just prior to the order being written up or the cash register ringing.

The word "sales" covers all the issues related to contacting your actual customers once you've established how to reach them through your marketing campaign. How will you train your sales staff to approach potential customers? Will you divide up your sales staff so some become experts in selling your bubble gum-scented bubble bath to small, independent, retail toy stores? Will other salespeople concentrate on developing relationships with major bubble gum manufacturers so the bubble bath could be sold in tandem, through their well-established national distribution outlets? Will you have a sales-force expert in buying television slots on Saturday morning cartoon shows or placing ads on the backs of kid-oriented cereal boxes?

What advertising and promotional efforts will you employ: two-for-the-price-of-one specials or free coupons inside those kid-oriented cereal boxes? Where can you locate lists of the greatest concentrations of children under the age of eight? What will you convey to children about your bubble bath that will convince them to ask their parents to buy it? Will you have to follow federal guidelines that require you to stick warning labels on every bottle to keep children from drinking your delicious-smelling soap?

In planning your sales activities, you will also need to answer questions such as: Is it ethical to contact your colleagues and clients from your former job as a door-to-door soap salesperson to tell them about your new bubble gum-scented bubble bath? Will you be the only salesperson in the beginning stages of your company? When will you know it's time to hire more sales staff? How do you convince your clients that your sales staff will take care of them as well as you did? What will your basic sales philosophy be—building long-term relationships with a few major clients, or developing a clientele of many short-term customers?

You will also need to consider how you will compensate your sales staff: with a base salary plus a commission, or in bottles of bubble gum-scented soap? Will you hire full-time staff with full benefits, or part-time staff without benefits? How will you motivate your staff to do the best sales job possible?

Knowledge of your competitive advantage is just as important in designing a dynamic sales effort as it is in developing an effective marketing campaign. You'll need to think about what product or service qualities will be the most compelling to your prospective customers. Then you'll have to devise convincing language that clearly communicates this competitive advantage to your sales staff, who will, in turn, use it when talking to your customers.

In my experience, the most important element of an effective sales effort is having a sales staff that thoroughly understands your business and the needs or your potential customers. Therefore, your sales plan must address the issue of how you will create a sales staff that is as knowledgeable about your business as it is about your potential customers.

Your bankable business plan must demonstrate that you are sales oriented by embracing the following concepts.

Get An Order Today—Or Yesterday

The most bankable business plan shows that you already have commitments for orders. Some very successful businesses have started with an order for a product even before there was a means by which to sell it. In 1975, a young entrepreneur discovered that IBM needed an operating system for the new personal computers they were eager to market in competition with an upstart company called Apple. The entrepreneur knew where he could obtain the right program, and made a deal with IBM before he even had the product in hand. His name was Bill Gates and the company he founded on that first sale was Microsoft.

Before you write your business plan, identify key potential customers, talk with them, and obtain commitments from them to buy when you're ready to sell. No other element will make your plan quite as bankable.

Make Sales A Priority For Everyone

Your plan should emphasize the belief that sales is a central function for virtually every employee and every department. You need to assure potential investors and lenders that you'll employ a team selling concept to address any possible questions from prospective customers. For example, if you're starting a software, consulting, or manufacturing company, you should take your technical people, not just your sales staff, to see prospective clients.

I saw a persuasive business plan for a currently successful restaurant that explained how the chef would leave the kitchen at least once a night to ask customers how they liked the food he had prepared. Making sales a priority works in the plan and it works in the business because it communicates to potential lenders and investors that attracting customers and keeping them happy is your top priority.

Never Delegate Yourself Completely Out Of Sales

Although most entrepreneurs recognize that they must be sales oriented, many don't actually enjoy selling. They may have started their ventures because they preferred to run the show, not sell the tickets, or they were excited about inventing a new computer application, not convincing people to try it. Many became entrepreneurs because they wanted the financial rewards of business ownership, but expected their products to virtually sell themselves. Because of their attitudes, some entrepreneurs structure their firms so that they are far from the front lines of selling. This is not just an organizational mistake, it's a costly error that can displease potential investors.

Many clients want to deal with the founder and head of the business because it boosts their egos to have that level of attention. Others believe they can get the best price and service only from top management. To attract and satisfy these potential customers, your plan must assure investors that you will not delegate all sales responsibility to others. Moreover, if you want to demonstrate throughout your organization (even if you employ only a few people) that sales is a top priority, you need to have contact with potential customers yourself.

Create The Right Ethical Environment

Selling is not about fooling someone into buying from you. Selling is about finding a long-term way to work together for the mutual benefit of both your business and your customers. If your approach to selling hinges on manipulation or being less than truthful, then your plan is built on shaky ground.

I am familiar with a large telecommunications company that enjoyed immediate success because it was well positioned as a low-cost provider in a rapidly growing market. When growth started to slow, the pressure from investors and top management for increased sales did not. The company's approach was to promise prospective clients the moon, but without a written agreement. This created a truly unethical environment that caused the best, most client-oriented salespeople to leave. When clients caught on to the ruse, they canceled their contracts and spread the word about the company's poor reputation. The company is now struggling to survive.

Your plan should stress that you are committed to developing and maintaining strong relationships with your customers by delivering what you promise and ensuring that everyone within your organization shares these ethical values. Establish this goal by your own example, by instituting professional sales training, by building your relationships with clients on the bedrock of honesty and by developing a strong competitive advantage based on product quality, good pricing, and unequaled service.

Be Highly Organized

By its nature, sales requires keeping track of multiple interactions with many current and potential clients. There are many software sales tracking programs such as ACT! or Goldmine, as well as database systems, such as Access, that can maintain your account lists and client interactions. In many cases, keeping a detailed notebook or a card file is sufficient.

Whatever system you use, the key is to be highly organized, so that you provide the proper followup and don't lose your customers in a chaotic mess.

Some systems give management a huge amount of data, from the number of sales calls made to the average order size. In my experience, this is useful information to some extent, but managers should not be fooled into believing that these statistics are as important as building long-term, mutually beneficial, client relationships achieved through in-person meetings. Establishing a few dependable and satisfied customers is almost always better than convincing clients to buy your product or service only once.

If your plan has a significant sales component—and most do—it's important to describe your sales system and objectives fully.

Compensate Based On Long-term Performance

Salespeople should earn financial rewards based on performance, but performance should be defined effectively. A commission based solely on sales, may, in fact, encourage staff to overpromise, or pressure clients into buying, or even to write up phony orders. I have worked with organizations that believed they were giving their salespeople the right incentives but, in reality, they were encouraging their staff to concentrate on hardsell, short-term, unethical techniques that eventually eroded customer trust and satisfaction, as well as future sales. You can assure potential investors and lenders that you understand these problems and can avoid them by stating in your business plan that you will:

* Pay commissions based on collections, not orders.

* Set long-term goals and give financial incentives for reaching them, instead of relying on weekly or monthly goals.

- Give salespeople a fixed financial base, so they're not under tremendous financial pressure to meet short-term quotas.

- Communicate your goal of building strong relationships with long-term clients.

- Recruit salespeople who are interested in working collaboratively with clients to help them meet mutually beneficial goals.

- Train your salespeople to deliver better service based on their understanding of client needs and goals.

Your Sales Force Can Be Your Competitive Advantage

Managing your sales force effectively will provide a major competitive advantage for your business—and it will make your business plan more compelling. Many entrepreneurs view their sales staff as an expensive, hard to manage, but necessary evil. If your sales staff is more client oriented, more knowledgeable about your product, and delivers better service than your competitor, you can build and maintain strong customer relationships. A well-designed sales effort can help bring in larger market shares than your competitors can achieve and it will keep business steady even during economic downturns. You can bank on it!

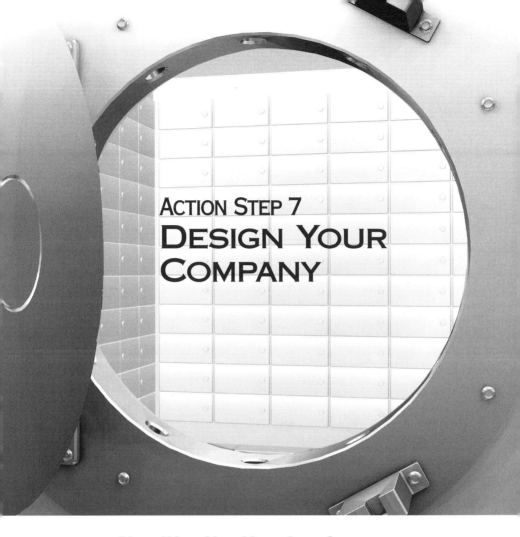

ACTION STEP 7
DESIGN YOUR COMPANY

HOW WILL YOU HIRE AND ORGANIZE YOUR WORKFORCE?

You have now defined your venture, its initial needs, targeted markets, and growth objectives. You have also described your marketing and sales strategies. Now, it's time to design the organizational structure that will enable your plan to become a real business. You may hope to run your company as one big happy family—and it may work out that way—but organizations require formal structure, and investors will expect to see these issues addressed in your plan.

This portion of your bankable business plan also establishes the staff structure that will be capable of implementing the strategies you have chosen to start your venture. In my opinion, the single greatest determinant of business success is implementation. We have all seen businesses fail because of the entrepreneur's inability to make dreams into reality.

An example I saw recently was a restaurant owner who failed to establish a chain of command between himself and his on-site manager. The manager was given a strict budget and decided he could only afford to hire poorly trained employees to wait on customers and cook in the kitchen. The new staff produced substandard food and provided mediocre service and the restaurant failed. Surely the owner didn't want this outcome but, by failing to design an organizational structure that created an effective chain of command and decision-making process, the restaurant was doomed. If you structure your business properly and can implement your plan effectively, you can succeed even against tough odds and rough competition.

By the time you've reached this stage of thinking about your potential business concept, you'll probably have a good idea of the number of people you'll need and the skills they'll require to get your enterprise up and running. Keep in mind that your initial plans will undoubtedly change as your business grows. You may need to hire more managers to supervise your expanding staff, or to set up new departments to meet new customer demands. Projected growth and expansion for your company should be mentioned in your business plan, but it's not the primary focus. For now, you want to secure help in getting started and convincing your funding sources that you will become profitable.

Let's imagine that you're the Field Center client who has identified a competitor's ocarina manufacturing plant to purchase. You have been running your grandfather's ocarina plant since his death, but the operation is still small and old fashioned. Buying the new plant will enable you to bring your manufacturing methods up-to-date and expand your customer base.

Investors will want to know if you're capable of running the show by yourself after you take over the plant. Do you need to bring in experienced managers right away? Will you keep some of the existing employees or hire all new people? And where do you find these potential employees?

Funding sources will also want to know if any of your partners expect to work alongside you, or if their obligations are only financial. How will you make changes at the new ocarina plant while maintaining the trust and cooperation of the employees you retain from your previous plant and the staff at the newly acquired plant? And how will you reassure both plants' customers that your new ocarinas will be as good as, if not better than, the ocarinas that used to roll off the assembly lines?

Your plan will need to specify the key management jobs and roles. Positions such as president, vice presidents, chief financial officer, and department managers should be defined along with stating who reports to whom. Running a manufacturing plant will require you to deal with dozens if not hundreds of employees, but what if you're someone who wants to build a better mousetrap? You will have some of the same issues, such as handling partners who may want to work side-by-side with you on your venture or convincing investors of your qualifications, but you may be the sole full-time employee for quite some time. How will you find the right consultants to advise you or the best vendors to supply your materials? Will you collect a salary? When will you know you need to hire a staff? What skills must they have? How do you recruit them? How will you structure your company so that the chain of command and quality control are maintained if the company grows dramatically?

And as soon as you have employees, you need to consider how you will handle their salaries and wages, their insurance and retirement benefits, as well as analyzing the extent of your knowledge of tax-related issues. As you think about hiring personnel and organizing your workforce, you must also confront your desire and ability to be a good boss. If you haven't contemplated this aspect of your commitment to owning your own company, now is the time to give it serious consideration.

Structuring Your Company

There are several basic designs for structuring your company, all of which can be depicted visually by an organization chart. Organization charts have the same two dimensions as maps. The north/south or vertical axis indicates power relationships. The higher up (more to the north) on the chart a position is, the more power that person controls. A person's boss usually appears above him or her on an organization chart. The east/west dimension specifies how tasks are assigned. Questions such as "Who covers Borneo?" or "Which department manages cuttlefish farms?" can be answered by looking horizontally, east to west, on the organization chart.

Organizations are defined by how the first level below the top is structured. Although you can mix and match organizational forms, most investors and lenders recognize five fundamental structures, which are described on the following page and depicted with their corresponding organization charts:

Product. These organizations have the first level below the top arranged according to products or product lines. Food companies generally organize this way, with each product having its own management team to oversee advertising, distribution, packaging, and promotions. This type of organization allows decision making to be placed at the product manager level.

PRODUCT ORGANIZATION

Geographical. Many companies, from car dealerships with locations just a few miles apart to airlines with operations on every continent, choose to organize geographically. This is most appropriate for businesses that need all the functions of the company within each geographical region. While the CEO and his staff in the central office will provide detailed oversight, each geographical division is a self-contained unit that operates independently.

GEOGRAPHICAL ORGANIZATION

Functional. In these organizations, the first level below the top is broken out by functions such as finance, sales, and manufacturing. Smaller organizations in stable businesses with a limited product line and routine technology are typically organized functionally. For example, a real estate management company would probably be organized functionally, having departments such as accounting, marketing, maintenance, and human resources.

FUNCTIONAL ORGANIZATION

Matrix. Matrix organizations are generally established in high-technology companies where specialized, technical teams work on solving specific problems related to complex, long-term projects. Matrix organizations tend to have team leaders, while each specialist also reports to the leader of the specialty. Companies that create complex products such as computers or airplanes usually organize this way, so that a manager can be assigned to develop a specific component or solve a particular problem, then pull the needed specialists into the team. The specialist, such as a physicist or meteorologist, reports to the team leader managing the specific task, as well as to the head of his or her specialty (such as physics or meteorology) within the company.

MATRIX ORGANIZATION

DASHED LINE REPRESENTS PROJECT COORDINATION

Hybrid. As its name implies, a hybrid organization combines elements of functional, product and geographical organizations. The chart shows that parts of the organization, such as the finance and distribution departments, are functionally structured, while other divisions, such as metal stamping or oil-drilling rigs, are organized by product. Hybrid structures combine the responsiveness of a product organization with the specialization and efficiency of a functional organization.

HYBRID ORGANIZATION

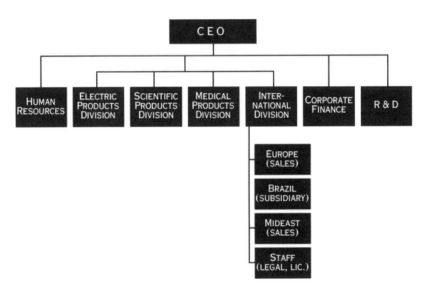

If your business requires an organization of a dozen or more people, it's wise to include a full organization chart along with your plan.

Means Of Control

If your plan calls for a sizeable organization, you will need to demonstrate that you will have the means to maintain control of your company. Here are some key means of control you should consider describing in your business plan:

Span of control is the number of people who report to one boss. This should be stated for organizations with large sales forces, manufacturing operations, or sizeable support departments, such as accounting.

Reporting tools are ways of keeping management informed of activities. These can be weekly staff meetings, memos, or sales-reporting systems. In manufacturing departments, where cost and efficiency are crucial, tracking systems that report on each employee's production may be needed.

Organizational culture is the atmosphere of morale and company spirit that exists among the staff. Creating the appropriate organizational culture is an important part of the success of many businesses.

Human Resource Management

Some businesses, such as fast food restaurants, function best by hiring short-term employees at low wages. Coping with the rapid turnover this policy engenders is part of the business plan. However, if hiring and retaining the right employees for the long term will be crucial to your company's success, you should describe your human resource management approach in your plan. Here are some issues to discuss:

Identify Key Employees

Business is a team sport and choosing your teammates may be the most important decision you make. The following template is useful in defining every key position in your organization:

- Title
- Job description
- Required degrees, training, and experience
- Compensation package, including salary, bonus, stock ownership, and stock incentives

- Résumés for current and prospective employees
- Strategies for positions that need to be filled

Design a Board of Directors or Board of Advisors

A significant element of your team can consist of people who are not full-time employees but who offer their expertise, experience, and contacts to support your business. A board of directors is a formal entity with ultimate legal control over the company and, potentially, personal liability for its actions.

A board of advisors is an informal group working to help the company, but without legal authority or any potential personal liability. Showing investors or lenders that you have recruited a high-powered, capable, and contributing group of directors or advisors will make your plan much stronger. For each proposed board member or advisor, I urge you to complete the same template as you would for key employees.

Establish Employee Compensation and Benefit Plans

Your approach to compensation and benefits should fit your overall strategy. If you're opening a fast food franchise, most of your employees will be young people who want a job, not a career, and see flipping burgers as a way to make money for tuition or a car. For these types of employees, a compensation plan that maximizes their paychecks at the expense of long-term benefits, such as pension plans, is probably best.

On the other hand, if you're building a consulting firm and want to keep your employees for the long run because they will maintain strong relationships with your clients, then a plan that stresses long-term benefits, such as health insurance, stock ownership, or pensions, is more attractive and effective.

Employee benefits is a complex, highly regulated, and rapidly changing area. You should consult with a benefits company or financial planner and receive actual proposals for employee benefits to include in your business plan.

Select Key Suppliers and Contractors

Henry Ford's first automobile plant functioned by funneling coal, iron ore, and other raw materials in one door and rolling finished Model Ts off the assembly line and out the other door. When Ford began his business, there were no suppliers of car parts, so his factory had to do it all.

In today's world, most companies subcontract out large portions of their essential processes. Dell assembles computers from components it purchases from hundreds of different suppliers. In certain cases, Toyota requires its suppliers to locate their facilities adjacent to the Toyota manufacturing plants so parts can be ordered and delivered within a few hours.

Chances are that your business plan will describe a venture more like Dell or Toyota than Henry Ford's original plant, and you will need to identify key suppliers.

Here are questions about suppliers that should be addressed in your plan:

- What materials will they actually be supplying?
- How long have they been in business?
- What are their credentials and track records?
- Why have you selected them? Price? Quality? Ability to supply an adequate quantity on time?
- Have they made a binding offer to supply certain products or services at a definite price?
- What is your backup plan if they don't do what they promised?

Suppliers with strong track records and excellent reputations will not only contribute quality materials to your business, they will also give your plan a powerful endorsement. If Intel has agreed to supply semiconductors for your product, investors and bankers will definitely take notice.

Legal Structures

Many entrepreneurs find choosing a legal structure for their businesses a daunting prospect and immediately hire a lawyer. A lawyer may be necessary at some point in establishing your venture, but legal services are not an expense you have to assume while preparing your business plan. Whether you hire a lawyer immediately or not, understanding the choices of legal structures is a good idea and, in fact, may not be as complicated as you think.

There are three considerations in choosing a legal structure for your venture:

Tax considerations. Some types of structure, such as limited partnerships, don't pay taxes directly, but pass profits and losses directly to their owners. The owners then pay taxes based on their own tax situations.

Liability considerations. Some structures, such as corporations, protect their owners from liability arising from actions of the company or its employees through what is known as the *corporate veil*. This protection is not perfect and, in cases of fraud or illegal activity, the corporate veil is pierced.

Investor considerations. The type and number of investors that you anticipate having for your venture is important because some structures, such as *S-corporations*, limit the number of possible investors. Others, such as general partnerships, have only one class of investors, while *C-corporations* allow for many. The option of having more than one class of investors means you can give varying voting or economic power to different groups of investors.

Once you analyze these considerations, you can match your needs with the types of legal entities available and make the best choice, from among these basic options:

Sole proprietorships have one owner who manages the business and contributes to the investment. There is no liability protection, and profits and losses are passed through directly to the owner's tax return.

General partnerships can have an unlimited number of partners, all of whom are collectively responsible for managing the business, contributing to the investment, and sharing in the profits. There is no liability protection, and profits and losses pass through directly to the partners' individual tax returns.

Limited partnerships have two classes of partners: *general* partners are responsible for the management of the business; *limited* partners are investors. General partners, however, can also invest as limited partners. Based on the profit-sharing agreement between the classes of partners, profits and losses pass through to the partners' individual tax returns. General partners have no personal-liability protection, but limited partners do.

C-corporations are usually the structure of choice for large companies. They can have an unlimited number of shareholders and an unlimited number of classes of stock. The shareholders have no personal liability. The company is managed by a board of directors, which can be held liable for the company's actions in certain cases. The corporation pays taxes on its profits. The profits then pass through to the shareholders in the form of dividends, which are then taxed again on the individual shareholders' tax returns.

S-corporations are taxed like partnerships, but provide the liability protection of a corporation. This allows profits and losses to pass through to the shareholders. There are some restrictions, for example the number of shareholders must be 75 or fewer, there can be only one class of stock, and all shares must be owned by only certain types of shareholders, such as individuals, trusts, or estates.

Limited liability companies allow for an unlimited number of investors, called *members*. Profits and losses pass through to the members' individual tax returns. The members cannot be held liable for actions of the company.

Limited liability partnerships and professional corporations are state-sanctioned forms of organizations that are designed for licensed professionals such as lawyers, accountants, doctors, and dentists. If you are preparing a plan for such a profession, you should ask your attorney about the advantages of using one of these legal structures.

Matching The Legal Structure With Your Investors

The number and characteristics of your investors may influence your choice of legal structure. Raising capital from private sources, such as family members, venture capital funds, or individuals is referred to as *private placements*, and will require a lawyer who is a specialist. The key concept here is called the *accredited investor*, which is an institution, such as an insurance company, a pension fund, or an investment firm. An accredited investor may also be an individual with a net worth in excess of $1 million, or an individual income of $200,000, or a joint income of $300,000 or more. When working with accredited investors to raise money for your business, you have much more flexibility than dealing with less wealthy and, therefore (according to the law), less sophisticated investors.

If you're aiming at this market of institutional or wealthy and sophisticated accredited investors, you need to produce a private placement memorandum and file it with the Securities and Exchange Commission (SEC), a process which requires the services of a securities lawyer. To raise money from the broader public, called an *initial public offering*, or IPO, requires a much more expensive and time consuming process of filing a prospectus with the Securities and Exchange Commission. With rare exceptions, this will require an experienced lawyer, if not a law firm, and an investment bank, or a consortium of investment banks, to sell the shares through the public market.

By analyzing the available legal structures, you will be able to choose the most appropriate method of organizing your potential business. This will help convince investors and lenders that you have researched the options, even if you haven't made a final decision or hired a lawyer. In fact, once you have established that you have considered this issue in your business plan, lenders and investors may offer helpful suggestions on choosing a legal structure.

Franchises

Some entrepreneurs believe that buying a franchise eliminates the need to prepare a business plan. The decision to buy a franchise certainly dictates many of the issues that your business plan must include, but it does not remove the necessity of having a plan. The most important issue in a franchise business plan is proving that the location you have chosen will be profitable.

Franchisors should provide potential franchisees with the basic business model for the franchise, including detailed cost estimates, average revenue for existing franchises, and typical financing structures. The plan for your specific franchise should cover:

A detailed analysis of local competition from other franchises for the same company, as well as for other competitive businesses.

A line-by-line comparison of the expenses that the franchisor projects with the local costs for your franchise. For example, if the franchisor gives you projections that include rent at $50 per square foot, you will need to demonstrate that you can obtain space at or below that amount.

An analysis of the franchise agreement that shows you have sufficient protections to ensure that no other franchises will be sold directly in your vicinity. Also, you should show that the franchisor is capable of fulfilling all promises, such as national advertising, or new product development, to keep your business viable.

Interviews with existing franchisees—who were *not* suggested by the franchisor—to substantiate the claims made by the franchisor, and to further demonstrate business viability.

The Key Question about Franchises

The key question to ask yourself about purchasing a franchise is: "Do I need to buy a franchise to be in this business?" Many people buy franchises because they like the idea of having a proven model for a business that comes with a template for operation. Others believe that a franchise has a greater chance of success than a non-franchise business. I don't believe that the evidence supports this. The major negative to franchises is cost. First, there is the price of purchasing the franchise. Second, there are the fees calculated from revenues that go directly to the franchisor.

It is not unusual for a franchise to pay 10 percent or more of its revenue to the franchisor in fees and mandated contributions to collective advertising. Think about how much of your profit is represented by these fees. The price of a great name-brand franchise may make these costs a bargain, but your plan still needs to address what you're getting from being a franchise relative to what you are paying.

Get a Franchise Lawyer on Your Team

The franchise area is a legal speciality unto itself. There are a surfeit of laws governing franchises, including many local regulations. You need to have a lawyer who is highly experienced in this area, and who can contribute advice as well as help you negotiate the terms of various agreements, including the franchise contract and leases. Place the lawyer and his or her credentials prominently in your plan.

Use the RMA Data

RMA data will give you important insights into a proposed franchise, and improve the quality of your plan. First, you can compare the franchisor's data with the RMA figures for similar non-franchise businesses. This research will help you analyze the profitability of buying a franchise, as opposed to starting your own business. Second, just as in any business, a comparison with industry averages for margins, financing, and operating costs is important in proving the reasonableness of your projections. Refer to Action Step 10 for a more detailed description of how to use the RMA data in creating a bankable business plan.

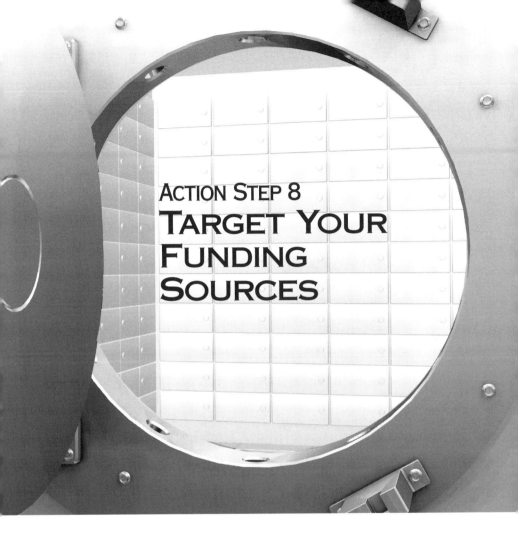

Action Step 8
Target Your Funding Sources

Where Will You Find Your Financing?

As your business concept takes shape, you should focus on the most likely financing sources. Issues such as the size of your business, the industry it is in, whether you are starting a new business or buying an existing one, and whether you can provide collateral to a lender must be considered in creating a target list of funding sources. Banks and other funding sources don't lend money because people with interesting business ideas are nice. They follow specific guidelines, such as the RMA data, which are designed to insure that they will make money by investing in or lending to your business.

For the vast majority of entrepreneurs, well known, high-profile means of raising money, such as from venture capital or by going public, are not viable options. Your own credit, credit rating, and business history are key factors in obtaining financing for your business through Small Business Administration (SBA) guaranteed loans and other bank credit options. Remember, the bank is essentially lending to you, not your business plan. Your ability to tap into your personal network of friends, family, and professional contacts is crucial to raising money beyond what your own personal funds or credit can provide. In all these cases, there are important considerations, such as the potential impact on relationships when family and friends become investors.

When you have completed this process of identifying the best potential funding sources for your business, you will be able to write a bankable business plan that addresses their issues and answers their questions, even before they ask them! Remember that a strong plan must meet the needs of financial supporters, whether they are bankers interested in prompt loan payments, investors who are looking for long-term profits, or family members who simply want you to have the chance to pursue your dream.

There are two main types of funding:

Debt is an agreement to borrow money and pay it back with interest. Types of debt include loans, mortgages, lines of credit, and leases. The bank, credit company, or individual lending the money usually requires collateral to cover the loan in case the borrower can't meet the payments. Common examples of collateral include real estate, equipment, and stocks. Debt with collateral is called *secured debt*. Debt is ranked by the order in which it is paid in the event of a default, liquidation, or bankruptcy. *Senior debt* is reimbursed first. *Junior* or *subordinated* debt is paid only after senior debt has been fully discharged.

Equity is ownership in a business. It can take the form of stock in a corporation or shares in a partnership. When you sell equity you are promising to give your investors a share of the profits from business operations or from an eventual sale of the business. Some equity investors require control of the companies they invest in and will want at least 51 percent of the stock, while others are content to be minority shareholders without ultimate control. In either case, stock sales in private companies usually involve a contract specifying the precise terms of the investment and the rights of the shareholders. These rights can vary greatly, but often include an option to buy more shares or force the company to buy the stock back within a certain time at a preset price. Creating such a shareholders' agreement requires an experienced lawyer who specializes in this area.

Potential Sources Of Financing

The sad fact is that you will probably have fewer options than you hoped for in financing your business, especially if you're planning a small, startup company. As options become more limited, your ability to finance your company becomes more important

Let's look at the potential sources for funding:

You. The truth is that about 90 percent of businesses start with the financial support of the entrepreneur. You should be prepared to make an investment by providing collateral, using your credit cards, or taking out personal loans to bring your idea to reality. Putting your own money into your business, or personally signing on loans that will require you to pay them back if the business cannot, is a huge step that you need to consider carefully. I have no doubt that you have a great deal of confidence in the likelihood of your venture's success, but the reality is that most new businesses fail. You have to decide in the most objective way whether you are prepared to sell your house, give up your retirement account, or even file for personal bankruptcy, if the worst happens.

Family and friends. Business and family are so tightly intertwined it is hard to separate them. More than two-thirds of all businesses involve two or more family members, have a manager who is a member of the family, and are majority-owned by family members. Next only to the entrepreneur, the family is the leading source of financial resources to start or grow a business. Relatives and close friends are a common source of financing for businesses because their agendas are more personal than business oriented—they want to help you succeed. Of course, they would like to share in your success, and they may see investing in your business as an opportunity to get in on the ground floor, but in my experience, these goals are secondary.

Family and friends make good investors because they are accessible and you can usually use your personal relationship to encourage their investment. The negative is that if the business fails, you will still be seeing them often!

I know of a fellow who started a moving company with investments from family members, including his parents and his father-in-law. The business failed despite his good efforts, because the city in which he had established his company experienced a sudden downturn in the economy. His parents treated the investment as a gift to their son. They told him they thought he did the best job possible, and they said they would invest again if he wanted to start another business in the future. His father-in-law, however, could never come to terms with his financial loss and raises it every time he sees his son-in-law.

There are several important lessons here. First, be selective about whom you ask for money, avoiding friends or relatives whose relationship with you might suffer too much if your business fails. Second, be sure to warn your investors of the real financial risk they are taking and give them every opportunity to say "no." Third, be prepared for the long-term negative consequences from some individuals, no matter how thoroughly they were warned, if your business *does* fail.

All these *caveats* notwithstanding, family and friends represent strong potential funding sources for most entrepreneurs.

Angels. Angels are wealthy individuals who invest directly in businesses. Although there are numerous web-based matching services linking entrepreneurs and potential angels, in my experience you are more likely to find an angel investor through an established personal or business relationship with an accountant, perhaps, or a lawyer who handles your business dealings. Angel investors tend to focus on industries they know through their direct experience or previous success. Most angels know exactly how much risk they are taking by investing in a startup or relatively new business, so they expect to earn high returns on their stake if the business becomes successful. Some will ask for a seat on your board of directors or for an option to purchase enough stock to control the company.

Making a deal with an angel is a bit like getting married—it requires careful thought before the actual commitment is made. Angel investors who are experienced in your industry will have strong ideas about how your business should be run. Unless these ideas closely match your own, you may be in for a long struggle. Many angel investors are also very tough negotiators when it comes to making a deal. They know how important obtaining financing is for you, because many have been in exactly the same position before, so be prepared for long and complex negotiations.

Venture capital firms. Venture capital firms are generally large, professionally managed funds. Many are organized as Small Business Investment Corporations (SBICs) which enables them to obtain SBA guarantees on part of their investment. Venture capital firms attract investment from pension funds, large corporations, and wealthy individuals.

Many entrepreneurs think that venture capital is a serious option for them, but, in reality, venture capital is a relatively small and highly specialized source of funding. Even in peak years, the venture capital industry makes fewer than 10,000 investments. In most cases, they are looking for large private companies with a strong probability of growth, in which they can invest several million dollars or more. They prefer to invest in companies that will provide a clear and profitable exit within a few years, such as going public or a merger with a larger company. Despite having invested in startups during the dot.com boom, venture capital firms rarely invest in new businesses. Generally, venture capital firms want to control the companies in which they invest.

Corporations. Occasionally, corporations will make direct investments in outside ventures. This is most often seen in technology industries, in which a large company, such as Intel, will invest in a small company that is developing a product Intel would eventually like to own. This type of investment is rare, and almost always carries an agreement to sell to the corporate investor at some point in the future if the investor wants to buy your product. It makes sense to look for this type of investor if you have personal contacts at a specific company, know your product would be very useful to them, and you feel comfortable becoming a division of the corporation in the future if you are successful.

Going public. To be blunt, for most businesses this is the equivalent of winning the lottery. Just look at the numbers. There are more than 10 million businesses in the United States, but only about 17,000 public companies. During the dot.com boom, many companies with little more than a cute logo were sold to the public. However, that period was an aberration and is now as faint a memory as most of the money that was invested. A company usually needs to have at least $20 million in annual revenue to be a candidate for a public offering.

Banks. Most banks focus on the financial record and strength of the individual entrepreneur when analyzing a loan application. Banks want the owner of the business to stand behind any loans by providing collateral to repay the loan if the business fails. If the company has a very strong record of profitability—and, therefore, the ability to pay interest and principal—or if the assets of the business are more than enough to secure the loan, this personal risk can sometimes be avoided. Most banks prefer making large loans over small loans, often with $50,000 as the cut-off point. This varies by bank, but the rule of thumb is that the smaller your request, the less likely it is to be viewed favorably at most banks.

How Banks Decide On Loans

With every loan, banks assume the risk that they might not be paid back. In addition to demanding collateral from either the loan applicant or a third party, banks manage this gamble by lending to low-risk, creditworthy people, by lending less than the customer is requesting, by charging higher interest rates and fees to compensate for accepting the risk and, most often, by not lending at all

Banks judge their loan decisions by looking at personal factors such as:

Your credit history. In this electronic age, lending sources can instantly evaluate how quickly and thoroughly you have paid your financial obligations. Late payments, delinquent loans, bankruptcies and how much credit you have been extended by banks, credit card companies, department stores, and credit bureaus, are all readily available to potential financial sources at the touch of a few computer keys.

Your character. A loan decision often comes down to a personal evaluation made by one or more loan officers. I've witnessed loans granted to entrepreneurs with bankruptcies in their past, and loans denied to people with stellar credit histories because the loan officer's sixth sense was triggered. This is so common that banks have a term for loans made to people without enough credit worthiness to sustain a loan. They're called character loans.

Your collateral. Nothing makes a banker happier than collateral to back up a loan. Mortgages are collateralized by the houses they finance and leases by the equipment being leased. Having collateral is a way for a bank to be repaid by seizing your assets if the loan is forfeited. Most lending sources require existing collateral, such as an entrepreneur's home or securities, before they grant small-business loans.

Your personal guarantee. Lending sources want to make entrepreneurs generally liable for the loan, not just the business they're starting. A personal guarantee provides this assurance without necessarily specifying the particular collateral. If you have few assets, a personal guarantee may not mean much, but if you have a home with significant equity value, or a large savings or investment account, giving the bank a personal guarantee will make the officers very happy, just as it should make you very nervous.

Your credit score. Some credit research firms, most notably Fair, Isaac and Company, calculate a single figure called a credit score. Factors such as your payment history, the amount of borrowing relative to your credit lines and recent inquiries by other financial institutions, are entered into a computer model that produces a single number, which is scored on a scale from a low of 400, representing poor credit, to a high of 900, representing strong credit.

Government loan guarantees. Federal agencies, such as the Small Business Administration, and various state programs help banks say "yes" to loans by agreeing to guarantee repayment of some portion of the loan, ranging from 50 percent to 90 percent. While these government loan guarantees carry a paperwork burden for both the entrepreneur and the lender, they encourage lenders to feel more comfortable approving loans. The presence of a government guarantee rarely stops a lender from asking for—and usually receiving—other collateral or personal guarantees for the loan. This gives bankers more than 100 percent in collateral and guarantees, and is rather like wearing both a belt and suspenders—unnecessary and unattractive, but it certainly keeps your pants up.

The best loan for any banker is one in which the business generates enough money to make the interest payments and, ultimately, return the entire amount of the bank's money. Government guarantees, personal guarantees, and collateral are just fallback positions in case the business fails and the entrepreneur defaults on the loan. Collecting from a guarantor or seizing and selling collateral generates a huge amount of work and aggravation for the bank, and marks the end of its business relationship with the borrower.

When a business performs as anticipated, meets its obligations, and grows to the point that its credit needs increase, the bank, the loan officers, and the entrepreneur have a win-win situation in which they can build a long-term, mutually beneficial business relationship. This partnership must begin with financial projections the bankers find credible and which prove to be credible. You want to have a strong credit score, show yourself to be of good character, and be able to offer as much in collateral or guarantees as are needed so the bank makes the loan, but financial performance and credibility are what truly matter.

Now that you understand the various funding sources, you can determine which funding source will be best for your business. Knowing this will allow your bankable business plan to address the issues that are most important to that funding source. Remember that a bankable business plan must meet the needs of financial supporters, whether they are bankers interested in prompt loan payments, investors looking for long-term profit, or family members who want to help you pursue your dream.

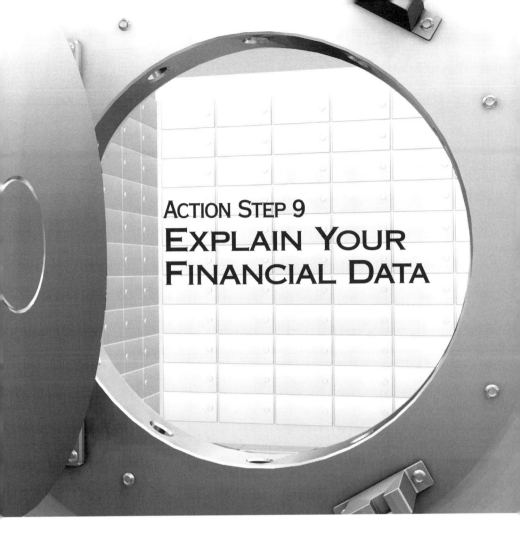

ACTION STEP 9
EXPLAIN YOUR FINANCIAL DATA

HOW WILL YOU CONVINCE OTHERS
TO INVEST IN YOUR ENDEAVOR?

The accuracy of your financial figures and projections is absolutely critical in convincing investors, loan sources, and partners that your business concept is worthy of support. The data must also be scrupulously honest and extremely clear. Since banks and many other funding sources will compare your projections to industry averages in the Risk Management Association data, your numbers will be more credible if they compare reasonably to the industry averages. If they don't, you should address this divergence thoroughly in your business plan. Action Step 10 explains how to complete this comparison, step by step.

The actual number-crunching portion of your business plan is not the place to talk about your pie-in-the-sky hopes for opening an ocarina plant in every country around the globe, or for convincing the U.S. Army that your squid-flavored pancakes should become standard fare in all military mess halls. It *is* the place to discuss how and why you need certain equipment, time, or talent; how much these items will cost; when you expect to turn a profit; and how much return and other benefits your investors will receive.

More new businesses fail because they simply run out of cash reserves than for any other reason. When projections are not met, investors lose confidence in the entrepreneur and the business, and become reluctant to invest more. Had the projections been less optimistic and the investors asked to invest more in the beginning, they probably would have done so. In most cases, proper planning and more accurate projections could have prevented this problem completely.

Start analyzing your financial information by going back to Action Step 2. Study your list of the tangibles and intangibles required to start your company and the costs you have estimated. Your business plan should clearly state the financing you need, how soon you require it, and how long before you start repaying investors. You should also explain what type of financing you hope to acquire, either *equity* (such as the sale of ownership shares in your company) or *debt* (such as loans to the company), and if you require capital expenditures to buy an automated pancake maker or working capital to pay for mousetrap design and market research.

If you're planning to buy an existing business, or already own a business you would like to improve or expand, you should provide a detailed historical financial summary of how well—or poorly—the business has done in the past. This analysis should also include a comparison of this venture's financial performance compared to the industry standards presented in the RMA data. Just as with your projections, the bank will likely perform a similar historical analysis anyway. If you do the comparison first, you show yourself to be diligent and savvy—and you can explain any differences between the company's performance and the RMA data in a way that reflects positively on your plans.

You should identify miscalculations you believe the previous owner might have made. Perhaps she put a great deal of money into producing gold-plated ocarinas that nobody wanted to buy. This is also the section of your business plan in which you should provide detailed figures on expected income, cash flow estimates, balance sheets, and future reasonable forecasts for your business. Do you hope to be producing 1,000 ocarinas per day in five years? Will you be able to lower the price of your better mousetraps once you can buy titanium by the ton? Are you planning to open three additional restaurants featuring squid-flavored pancakes?

By the time you've pulled together all the important financial data, you'll have a clearer picture of how much of your own funds you'll be able to commit, the amount of money you'll need to borrow, and the number of investors you'll have to secure. This is also a good time to take a crash course in accounting principles or learning how to create spread sheets on a computer program. No matter what business you intend to start, you will need to know how to analyze not only projected profits and losses, but actual profits and losses as soon as your first customer walks through your pancake house door or buys a bottle of your bubble gum scented bubble bath.

The Essential Financial Statements

With the presentation of your financial data you are addressing the fundamental reason why virtually all businesses exist: to earn money. Your financial data must include the following elements:

Income statements are summaries of an existing company's performance over a period of time. They are usually prepared using the *accrual system*, which recognizes revenues when they are earned and expenses at the time goods or services are con-sumed—not when the revenue is received or the expenses are paid. *Projected income statements* are called *pro forma income statements* and are an absolute requirement for any business plan.

Balance sheets are statements that present the financial status of an existing or projected business at a particular point in time. An overview of a company's capital position, such as how much debt it owes and the value of its assets, is located on the balance sheet.

Cash flow projections are income statements revised to show the anticipated actual inflows and outflows of money. *Operating cash flow* is the cash flow from the operations of the business such as manufacturing hats or building tree houses. *Net cash flow*, which is what one sees on the *statement of sources and uses*, includes other sources or uses of cash, such as sales or purchases of assets and investment performance. A company's cash flow can differ significantly from what the income statement shows. Because keeping adequate cash reserves is necessary for the company to continue to operate, the cash flow projections are essential. Generally, cash flow statements differ from income statements in the following ways:

Revenue shows up on the cash flow statements when payment is received, which, for most businesses, is between 30 and 90 days after bills are sent out.

Expenses are recorded on cash flow statements when they are actually paid, not when the product or service is billed, which is usually 30 or 60 days after the bill is received.

Depreciation, which is recorded as an expense on the income statement, is not a cash item and therefore is not included on the cash flow statement.

Principal payments on loans or purchases of stock from shareholders are included as a use of cash on the cash flow statement, but are not seen on the income statement.

Statements of sources and uses show the actual sources and the uses of money by combining information from the *profit and loss statement* and balance sheet. Sources of funds typically include investment, increases in loans, and profits. Uses include items such as investment in equipment, loan repayments, dividends, and operating losses.

Debt-management schedules are projections that indicate your company's ability to pay interest and principal in accordance with your loan agreements. It is absolutely critical that the projections show that the company's obligations to its lenders will be met. Failure to do so will result in the company's credit being reduced, and can eventually lead to foreclosure and bankruptcy. An essential financial projection is a separate statement or table that shows the interest payment and principal repayment schedule and the company's ability to pay them. Since payments are made from cash flow, the cash flow statements must show what percentage of cash flow is going to make payments and how much cash the company still has after paying its debt obligations.

Returns analysis is a statement that shows the projected financial returns on the investment in your company. Potential investors always ask "How much money will I make?" The answer is found in the returns analysis, which shows potential investors how much they will earn through current payments such as dividends or by distributions from the sale of stock or the company as a whole. Whatever your particular strategy for producing returns for your investors is, the plan needs to show it and calculate what the returns will be.

The returns analysis adds profit distributions and the value of the equity in the business and compares it to the investment made. Thus, $1 million invested in year one, earns 50 percent annually if it is worth $2 million in year three (two years later). A returns analysis requires that estimates of the value of the company be completed.

If your plan is to sell the business in a few years, the returns will largely be a function of the value of the company at the time it is sold. If, on the other hand, your plan is to own your business for a long time, the returns will largely be a function of profit distributions over time to the shareholders.

Schedules of investment and capital expenditures are lists of the amounts of money that need to be spent on items with long usable lives. The initial startup of your business, either by purchasing an existing company or founding a new one entirely from scratch, requires investment. A schedule that details this initial investment, including items such as legal expenses, equipment, banking fees, and rent deposits, is essential. Every year of operation results in further capital expenditures for new equipment, buildings, or product development. This should also be presented in the schedules of investments and capital expenditures, the total of which is then carried over to the cash flow statement.

Break-even analysis answers several key questions, including how much revenue your business will need to break even, what your fixed costs are, and how much the business will earn on every dollar of sales after breaking even. Not only are these figures extremely useful for your own understanding of your business, but you can expect potential lenders and investors to ask these questions as well.

The key to preparing a break-even analysis is separating your costs into fixed costs and variable costs. Fixed costs remain the same, regardless of your revenue. These include items such as salaries, rent, interest payments, and insurance. Variable costs go up with greater revenue and include items such as costs of raw materials, royalties, shipping, and costs of returns. Basic introductory accounting books will take you through this process in greater detail. I suggest a few in the Resources at the end of the book.

Examples of financial statements, for a fictional company

called Lightning Larry's, Inc., are located at the end of this Action Step, where you'll also find guidance as to how to produce them.

The Six Key Financial Assumptions

The six key financial assumptions provide the foundation for projections, and should be clearly listed along with them. The test of complete financials is whether someone can read them and fully understand them without having to ask you questions. In my experience, you can pass this test if you take the time to fully explain your assumptions. Of course, you need to be careful about all your financial estimates. Mistakes undermine the confidence of anyone who reads your plan. These key financial assumptions are critical—mistakes here will not just erode confidence, but will probably doom your efforts:

Financial Assumption 1: Startup costs. No matter how profitable a business you expect to have, if you overpay to start it, it just won't work. I've seen this problem every day on both a large and small scale. Daimler-Benz's purchase of Chrysler and Hewlett-Packard's purchase of Compaq, are examples of this on a large scale.

On a smaller scale, the famous Russian Tea Room next to Carnegie Hall in New York City flourished for decades through good and bad economic times. After purchasing the restaurant for $6.5 million, the new owners spent four years and $36 million(!) on a lavish renovation. Within two years after its grand reopening, the owner filed for bankruptcy and the Russian Tea Room closed its ornate doors. This New York icon reopened in November of 2006, I hope under the care of wiser stewardship.

The components of startup costs include:

- Acquisition price of buying an existing business.
- Capital investment in land, building, renovations, and equipment prior to starting operations.

• Operating losses during the startup phase, which usually arise prior to achieving sales goals and heavy, initial marketing expenses.

Financial Assumption 2: Revenue projections. All the entrepreneurs I have advised believed that their biggest problem would be handling the volume their businesses would generate, with customers beating a path to their doors. Reality is quite different, as most experienced entrepreneurs will attest. Generating first-time orders is one of the toughest assignments in business, and building and expanding a list of customers is a close second. The great difficulty with revenue projections is that for many people they are pulled out of thin air. The solution to this is twofold:

Anchor revenue projections to reality by using techniques such as supplying lists of potential customers, pretesting your products or services through surveys or focus groups, comparing your product's features and price to the existing competition, and by comparing your revenue projections to industry averages or to similar businesses that you know.

Be conservative in the extreme. After you have created projections that you are certain approximate reality, cut them mercilessly. Based on what I have seen, when revenue projections seem ludicrously low to the entrepreneur, they are approaching reality!

Financial Assumption 3: Operating costs. Calculating potential expenses after startup requires a tremendous amount of work. To make certain you have covered each item, use the following as a checklist:

Estimate every cost from fixed costs, such as rent, utilities, advertising, employees, and employees' benefits, to variable costs, such as raw materials, shipping your products, and commissions to your salespeople. These are used in the break-even analysis which was discussed earlier in this chapter.

Set up your statements of costs with as many categories as you can imagine and provide an explanation of how each estimate was determined so that people who question your numbers can follow your process. Providing this backup to your numbers helps establish you as a thorough manager who will inspire confidence in funders and investors.

Build in contingencies for issues such as additional advertising, legal expenses, traveling to meet with customers, and terminating employees who don't work out. After making these provisions, add a general contingency number of at least 5 percent to your total estimated expenses.

Financial Assumption 4: Borrowing. You need to speak with lenders about their particular guidelines for lending to your specific type of business, which is covered in Action Step 8. One of the great mistakes that entrepreneurs make is assuming that they will get a bank to lend them more than it usually does. Banks have precise guidelines and rarely deviate from them. The RMA data, described in Action Step 10, is a great resource to help you determine how much, on average, banks lend to businesses such as yours. Your financial projections need to show how much more cash flow the company will have than interest costs and how much more cash reserves it will have than are required for principal payments.

Financial Assumption 5: Equity returns. The amount of investment you are seeking in the form of stock or partnership shares requires that you project credible returns to investors. Because equity investors earn money from company profits and from the increase in the company's value, these figures must be calculated based on how much investors will put in and how much they will get back. Following these calculations, a return on investment can be determined and shown. If the return looks like a number you might earn from a bank savings account, you need to rethink the deal.

Financial Assumption 6: Company value. Tracking your company's estimated worth should appear throughout the entire period of your projections. Investors and lenders want to know where *they* stand, and you need to know where *you* stand at any given point if the company folds or is sold. Calculating the company's value depends a great deal on the industry. Some businesses, such as restaurants, sell for the value of their real estate, leases and fixed assets. Technology companies, such as manufacturers of high-tech medical products, will sell as a multiple of their revenue, while media companies, such as magazines, will sell for a multiple of annual cash flow. Some businesses, such as a one-person consulting firm, will sell for little because there is no assurance that clients will move to the new owner.

Typical financial methods of calculating a company's value include estimating profits for the next ten or fifteen years and then calculating the *net present value*, or current cash equivalent of this stream of profits. Lenders will often ask businesses to calculate *book value*, which is assets minus liabilities. You need to do the research in your industry to come up with a company valuation to use in your financial projections.

How To Create Statements

Many people are intimidated by the prospect of producing financial projections. However, if you manage the process by breaking it down into its components, doing what you can do best, finding resources to make other parts easier, and bringing in professionals to help with the remaining pieces, it can actually be a great way to learn a huge amount about the financial aspects of your business.

Build the structure of your statements. By now, you should have copies of financial statements from companies that are in your industry. You may have obtained these from your lawyer, accountant, industry trade group, industry reference book, such as those listed in the resources for Action Step 4. If you have not been able to obtain such sample statements, you can use standard statement formats from an accounting book or from one of the websites listed in the resources for Action Step 9. You may also follow the statement formats for Lightning Larry's, Inc. at the end of this Action Step or in the sample plan at the end of the book.

Start filling in the blanks. Now, do the best you can to fill in the blanks. In my experience, most people are able to do very well creating a statement of estimated startup costs, income statements, cash flow projections, and debt-management schedules. The key technical accounting issues are the differences in the timing of expenses and revenue between the income statement and the cash flow statement. The income statement recognizes income based on an accrual system, which is when the income is earned or expenses incurred, and the *cash flow statement* recognizes income when it is received and expenses when they are paid.

Statements of sources and uses and balance sheets have more technical accounting issues to manage. If you cannot complete the statements yourself, take advantage of the resources listed at the back of the book, or get professional help.

Use some outside help. If you are not experienced enough to prepare statements yourself, I suggest you consider one of the following options:

Use one of the templates from the website: www.bankablebusinessplans.com. Quicken and Quickbooks also offer statement templates.

Obtain technical assistance from a small business development center or other type of entrepreneurship center. Once you have researched good estimates and produced statements as well as you can, the rest will not be a big job for an experienced professional.

Ask your accountant for help in finishing the statements. As you will probably want to keep the expenses down, I suggest this as a last resort. Do as much as you can yourself before seeing the accountant, and get a fixed price from the accountant to finish the statements before you agree to use her services.

Following are the Essential Financial Statements for the fictional company Lightning Larry's, Inc.

**Essential Financial Statements For
Lightning Larry's, Inc.**

Lightning Larry's, Inc.

Income Statement

	Year 1
Revenue	**$1,200,000**
Cost of Goods Sold	(180,000)
Estimated Gross Profit	**1,020,000**
Expenses	
Employees	220,000
Owner's Salary	60,000
Payroll Taxes	32,400
Supplies	5,200
Insurance	22,500
Rent	16,000
Promotion	9,000
Advertising	6,000
Telephone & Utilities	11,250
Professional Fees	4,500
Miscellaneous	11,300
Operating Expenses	**398,150**
Interest	81,940
Depreciation	45,000
Total Expenses	**525,090**
Estimated Profit before Taxes	494,910
Taxes	(0)
Net Profit after Taxes	**$ 494,910**

Depreciation of $315,000 over 7 years

Lightning Larry's, Inc.

Cash Flow Statement

	Year 1
Cash Receipts	**$900,000**
Cost of Goods Sold	(180,000)
Estimated Gross Profit	**720,000**
Expenses	
Employees	180,000
Owner's Salary	40,000
Payroll Taxes	28,000
Supplies	3,700
Insurance	12,500
Rent	12,000
Promotion	7,500
Advertising	4,000
Telephone & Utilities	9,650
Professional Fees	3,200
Miscellaneous	9,000
Operating Expenses	**309,550**
Cash Flow (EBITDA)	410,450
Depreciation	45,000
Amortization of Loans	101,526
Cash Flow (EBIT)	**$263,924**

Lightning Larry's, Inc.

Year 1 Balance Sheet

	Year 1
Assets	
Current Assets:	
Cash & Cash Equivalents	$ 54,775
Accounts Receivable	248,035
Other Short-Term Assets	0
Total Current Assets	302,810
Fixed Assets:	
Furniture & Equipment (cost)	$ 315,000
Goodwill	1,606,674
Equipment	22.500
Less Accumulative Depreciation	(45,000)
Total Fixed Assets	1,899,174
Other Assets:	0
Total Other Assets	0
Total Assets	2,201,984
Liabilities & Stockholders' Equity	
Current Liabilities:	
Accounts Payable	58,600
Short-term Bank Borrowing	0
Other Short-term Liabilities	0
Total Current Liabilities	58,600
Non-current Liabilities:	
Seller Note	448,055
Long-term Bank Debt	400,419
Total Non-current Liabilities	848,474
Stockholders' Equity:	
Common Stock	800,000
Retained Earnings	0
Income	494,910
Total Stockholders' Equity	1,294,910
Total Liabilities & Stockholders' Equity	**2,201,984**

Lightning Larry's, Inc.
Year 1 (Includes Purchase and 1 Year of Operation)
Statement of Sources and Uses of Funds

Uses		Sources	
Purchase of Assets	1,500,000	Bank Loan	450,000
Less Expenses for			
Purchase	15,000	Owner's Investment	800,000
Working Capital	50,000	Seller Note	500,000
Interest Payments	81,940	Cash Flow (EBITDA)	410,450
Loan Amortization	101,526	Decrease in	
		Working Capital	38,016
Total Uses	**1,748,466**	**Total Sources**	**1,748,466**

Bank Note Calculations

Loan Amount	$450,000
Annual Interest Rate	8.25%
Loan Period (Years)	7
Start Date of Loan	9/1/07
Scheduled Monthly Payments	$7,069.98
Scheduled Number of Payments	84
Total Interest	$143,878.03

Seller Note Calculations

Loan Amount	$500,000
Annual Interest Rate	10.00%
Loan Period (Years)	7
Start Date of Loan	9/1/07
Scheduled Monthly Payments	$8,300.59
Scheduled Number of Payments	84
Total Interest	$197,249.73

Lightning Larry's, Inc.
Ratios

Type

Current	0.84
Quick	0.84
Sales / Receivables	12.00
Cost of Sales / Inventory	N.A.
Cost of Sales / Payables	0.00
Sales / Working Capital	24.00
EBIT / Interest	1.00
Net Profit + Depreciation, Amortization / Currently Maturing Long-term Debt	N.A.
Fixed / Worth	1.47
Debt / Worth	0.66
% Profit Before Taxes / Tangible Net Worth	0.38
Profit before Taxes / Total Assets	0.22
Sales / Net Fixed Assets	0.63
Sales / Total Assets	0.54
%Depreciation, Amortization / Sales	N.A.
Officers', Directors', Owners' Comp. / Sales	23.33
Return on Equity	0.25

Notes: Slash (/) denotes "divided by." Because company provides a service, and does not maintain physical inventory, ratios that include inventory or depreciation calculations related to inventory are Not Applicable (N.A.).

Lightning Larry's, Inc.

Returns Analysis – End of Year 1

Purchase Price	$1,500,00
Owner's Equity	800,000

Company Value at End of Year 1

EBITDA	410,450
Sale Multiple	4.5
Company Value	**1,847,025**

Less:	
Seller Note	448,055
Bank Loan	400,419
Net Proceeds	**998,551**

Change in Owner's Investment	**$198,551**
Rate of Return	**24.82%**

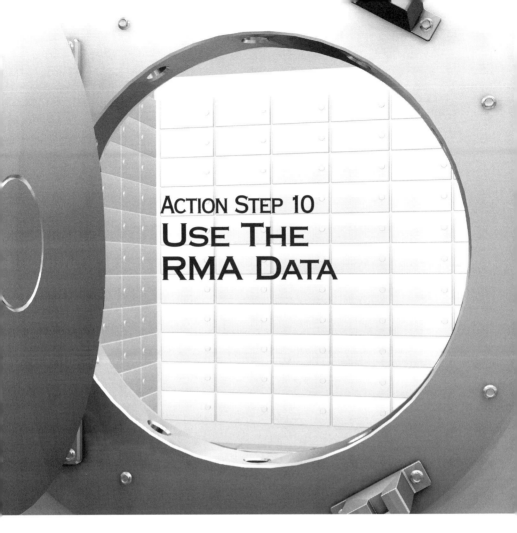

ACTION STEP 10
USE THE
RMA DATA

CHECK YOUR ANSWERS
AGAINST THE ANSWER KEY

Now that you've learned how to create a credible, thoughtful, detailed, conservative, and properly presented bankable business plan, you're prepared to apply the advantage of the Risk Management Association data. Most potential lenders and investors will compare your projections with the data supplied by the RMA, an association of over 3,100 banks and other financial institutions that pool their business clients' financial data.

As its name implies, the purpose of the RMA is to help its members limit risk by avoiding loans to businesses whose numbers are inaccurate or unrealistic. The RMA data serves as an answer key against which bankers can double check the financial projections of any business plan in any type of industry. If you compare your figures to the RMA data *before* you submit your business plan to potential lenders or investors, you will improve your chances of achieving the financial support you need to start your business.

No matter how high your credit score, or how many government guarantees you can produce, or how much collateral you can offer, there is no replacement for credible, accurate projections. Some bankers will simply pass on making a business loan if the projections are not convincing. Others will decline to make a business loan, but will offer to make a personal loan if your collateral or guarantees are strong enough. Neither of these options should be as attractive to you as obtaining a business loan, which reduces your personal risk and builds your company's credit.

While virtually all banks and many other funding sources use the RMA data, few entrepreneurs take advantage of this significant resource, but you can. I strongly urge you to do so. The RMA data may seem intimidating at first, because the publication you will use, *Annual Statement Studies,* looks like the Manhattan telephone directory. It's actually quite straightforward and easy to decipher. I will guide you through the process of finding the right data for your business plan and using it to your advantage.

Most libraries with some focus on business, and virtually all Small Business Development Centers, have the RMA's *Annual Statement Studies.* Since you will need copies of only a few pages, it is not difficult to obtain the data you need this way, and the cost is minimal. The RMA also sells their data over their website, one category at a time, for a cost of $110, at *www. rmahq.com.* However, I find the RMA book easier to use than the RMA website.

Working With The RMA Data

Suppose you want to open a florist shop, and have written a plan that includes detailed financial projections. You look in the

RMA data for florists and find the category for sales that covers your own projections. Let's say that you're projecting $1.5 million in annual sales. This will guide you to the data for florists with between $1 million and $3 million in sales. The RMA reports that florists of this size have an average margin on sales of 56 percent, which means they sell flowers for about twice what they pay for them. If you project that you will sell flowers for three times what you pay for them, you need to explain this discrepancy. Perhaps you'll sell only fancy floral displays, and the margin is higher for those than it is on cut flowers sold by the bunch. If, on the other hand, there is no explanation, you will need to take a new look at your projections and revise them.

The RMA data includes information that relates business profits to the amount of interest that florists pay. The average florist in the RMA database has three times as much in operating profits (called *EBIT*, or Earnings Before Interest and Taxes) as interest costs. I would say that if you are projecting less than two times as much operating profit, or EBIT, as interest you should revisit your projections and revise the amount of funding you expect to receive.

Once you perform the same comparison for the other key figures explained here, you'll be in great shape to present your numbers to the bank.

Locate the page that pertains to your business by using the SIC or NAICS codes. The RMA data is organized by a government system called *SIC*, or *Standard Industrial Classification*, that categorizes all businesses. There are two complications that you need to know about. The first is that a newer system, called *NAICS*, *North American Industrial Classification System*, is replacing SIC, which has become out of date. The simplest and fastest way to find the right code is to look through the *Annual Statement Studies'* table of contents.

The second complication is that it might not be obvious which code is best for your business. For example, if your business is a retail bakery with a line of prepackaged baking products that are sold in other stores, you could choose the SIC for retail bakery or the one for bakery products manufacturing. In these cases, you may want to present both sets of RMA data for comparison purposes. Or you can choose the RMA data that by comparison shows your business in the best light.

How you choose to categorize your business may have an impact on lenders. For example, if the bank has told you that they are less inclined to lend to retailers than to manufacturers, then choose the category that will appeal to them the most.

Find the column that matches your business size. There are two pages for florists. One page sorts the florists by the amount of assets reported on the florists' financial balance sheets. Ignore that page for now, because it is easier to look at the next page which sorts the florists based on their annual revenue. Find the column that most closely matches the sales you project. This column of numbers is all you will need for your comparison.

Place your numbers next to the RMA numbers. In Action Step 9, I explain which pieces of financial information are most important to a banker or investor. You will see that I've organized these items so that they match the items in the RMA data. Now, your projections and the RMA data can be easily compared. All the numbers and ratios that you will need to compare to the RMA data can be created from the financial projections you prepared earlier. Clearly, startups will have to present forecasted numbers without financial history.

Explain the differences between your data and the RMA data, or adjust your projections. If your projections closely match the RMA data or are more conservative than the RMA data, you have nothing more to do, other than to point this out proudly to your potential funders. If your projections are more optimistic than the RMA data, you need to explain this discrepancy in the text of your plan.

The Answer Key Revealed

Although the RMA's *Annual Statement Studies* is thick, there is only one column of numbers that will be of importance to you. This is the column that contains 81 numbers gleaned from businesses of similar size to yours on the page that presents your industry. Of these 81 numbers you probably need to compare only 16 to see whether or not your numbers will pass the bankers' test. You'll find these 16 numbers referenced on the sample RMA data pages that follows this Action Step.

There are two RMA pages for each industry. One presents the data sorted by the amount of sales and the other by the amount of assets the business has. Two considerations should guide your decision on which one to use for your comparison. First, some businesses, such as consulting firms or real estate agencies, have few physical assets. So using data sorted by sales is best. On the other hand, a business such as a manufacturing plant with lots of valuable physical assets is best compared to businesses that are sorted by asset size. Second, use data from larger samples. The first full line in each column tells you how many businesses make up the group sampled for the data in that column. So if the relevant sample sorted by sales is only 15, but the relevant group sorted by assets is 90, use the latter.

Here are the most significant financial figures to compare to yours. The numbers at the beginning of each paragraph correspond to the highlighted numbers on the sample RMA pages at the end of this Action Step.

1. Trade Receivables (net): How much your business is owed by its customers, with a reasonable allowance for accounts that will never pay. Some industries, such as fast food restaurants, have almost no receivables, while other industries, such as contractors who sell to government agencies, have huge receivables. If your assumption is more optimistic than the industry norm, you may find yourself running short of cash. And running short of cash closes more businesses than anything else.

2. Notes Payable–Short-term and **3. Long-Term Debt** together represent how much money your business owes. Notes Payable (Short-term debt) generally have a term of one year or less. Long-Term Debt has a term longer than one year. Since a bank's loans are usually made in the form of long-term debt, a banker will be very attentive to your projections here.

The group of numbers labeled "Income Data" includes:

4. Net Sales are Gross Sales less Returns and Discounts.

5. Gross Profit is Net Sales minus the cost of the items or services you sold.

6. Operating Profit is Gross Profit minus the Operating Expenses. Operating Expenses includes all selling, administrative, and depreciation costs (but not interest expense). The category "All Other Expenses" covers interest and miscellaneous expenses not included in Operating Expenses.

7. Profit Before Taxes is the business's profit after all expenses, including interest, are subtracted (but not taxes!).

Ratios are calculations used to evaluate business performance. The RMA data presents three numbers for each ratio: the average of the top quartile of businesses, the median ratio for the entire sample, and the average for the bottom quartile. Presenting the numbers this way gives you a sense of the average (median) and the range for each ratio. All ratios are used as indicators of potential problems. When a ratio seems too far from the norm, it usually signals the need for further analysis.

The key ratios are:

8. Current Ratio is Current Assets (generally the company's cash, receivables, inventory) divided by Current Liabilities (generally short-term loans and upcoming loan payments, payables, and taxes currently owed) and is a rough indication of a company's ability to pay its current obligations. The higher the ratio, the stronger the company.

9. Quick Ratio, or **Acid Test,** is Cash and Equivalents (such as money market accounts the company may have) plus Receivables minus allowances for non-paying accounts divided by Current Liabilities. This is a similar, but stricter, measure of a company's ability to pay its bills.

10. Sales divided by Receivables (invoices that your company has sent out but has not yet been paid) gives a measure of turnover or how many days on average it takes your customers to pay. The higher this number, the fewer days on average for your customers to pay.

11. Cost of Sales divided by Inventory (items waiting to be sold) measures how often your inventory turns over in a year. A fruit store turns over its inventory every week or less. An antique store turns over its inventory a few times a year. A high ratio can mean efficient use of inventory or it might mean that a company starved for cash has cut its inventory to the bone.

12. Cost of Sales divided by Payables (bills received but not paid) shows how quickly a business pays its bills. A high ratio means that bills are being paid promptly. A low ratio may indicate a company that is experiencing a cash shortage and is paying its suppliers too slowly.

13. EBIT (Earnings Before Interest and Taxes) divided by Interest shows the ability to pay interest. It is unusual to see this ratio below 2 for small businesses.

14. Net Profit plus Depreciation and Amortization divided by the Current Portion of Long-Term Debt shows an ability to pay similar to EBIT, but for scheduled principal repayments. Depreciation is a non-cash item that is usually calculated by your accountant to reflect how your company's long-term assets are used over time. Amortization is the payment of the principal part of your company's loans.

15. Fixed/Worth (Net Fixed Assets divided by Tangible Net Worth) shows what percentage of the long-term assets, such as a manufacturing plant and equipment, have been paid for by the owners' investment. The lower the ratio, the more it appears that the owners have invested in their company for the long term.

16. Debt/Worth (Total Liabilities divided by Tangible Net Worth) shows the relationship between the owners' and the lenders' capital. The higher the ratio, the less the owners have put in the company relative to the lenders.

It Really Is That Simple

Producing a meticulous set of financial projections and comparing them to the RMA data, along with either explaining or reducing the differences, will result in a banker or investor who says "Your numbers look good." This is the best possible reaction, and one you can achieve by plugging the RMA numbers into your spreadsheets and using the definitions above to explain the numbers like an expert!

The following are RETAIL–Florists data pages (reduced to fit this book) from the RMA's *Annual Statement Studies*. The white numbers in the black circles correspond to the sixteen most significant financial figures that were referenced in this action step.

RETAIL—Florists   NAICS 453110   (SIC 5992)

Current Data Sorted By Assets | **Comparative Historical Data**

Type of Statement	0-500M	500M-2MM	2-10MM	10-50MM	50-100MM	100-250MM	4/1/00-3/31/01 ALL	4/1/01-3/31/02 ALL
Unqualified			1				1	2
Reviewed		2	4				4	4
Compiled	9	3	2				27	24
Tax Returns	27	7	2			2	20	20
Other	5	6	3	1			17	10
		27 (4/1-9/30/04)			47 (10/1/04-3/31/05)			
NUMBER OF STATEMENTS	41	18	12	1		2	69	60
ASSETS	%	%	%	%	%	%	%	%
(1) Cash & Equivalents	11.3	12.4	7.9				14.0	10.9
Trade Receivables (net)	15.3	16.2	10.7	D A			17.0	18.8
Inventory	23.8	18.3	18.6	T A			23.4	22.3
All Other Current	1.5	1.6	3.7				2.1	3.1
Total Current	51.8	48.6	40.8	N O			56.5	55.1
Fixed Assets (net)	32.6	40.1	42.6	T			32.7	33.2
Intangibles (net)	5.9	4.6	9.9				4.6	5.2
All Other Non-Current	9.7	6.8	6.7				6.2	6.4
Total	100.0	100.0	100.0				100.0	100.0
LIABILITIES				A V A I L A B L E				
(2) Notes Payable-Short Term	14.0	3.9	7.0				6.0	8.6
Cur. Mat.-L/T/D	15.1	4.7	2.9				5.2	6.5
Trade Payables	26.6	15.3	9.7				21.2	20.8
Income Taxes Payable	.1	.1	.2				.2	.2
All Other Current	15.3	4.1	7.9				19.5	16.8
Total Current	71.0	28.1	27.6				52.2	52.9
(3) Long-Term Debt	34.7	25.1	18.7				28.9	34.4
Deferred Taxes	.1	.3	.3				.3	.3
All Other Non-Current	17.3	3.2	8.5				6.4	2.9
Net Worth	-23.1	43.3	44.9				12.2	9.5
Total Liabilities & Net Worth	100.0	100.0	100.0				100.0	100.0
INCOME DATA								
(4) Net Sales	100.0	100.0	100.0				100.0	100.0
(5) Gross Profit	57.5	49.9	61.5				52.8	52.5
Operating Expenses	55.1	48.5	62.0				51.9	50.9
Operating Profit	2.3	1.5	-.5				.8	1.6
(6) All Other Expenses (net)	.2	-.3	.0				.1	.9
(7) Profit Before Taxes	2.1	1.8	-.5				.7	.7
RATIOS								
(8) Current	1.8 / 1.0 / .4	2.6 / 1.9 / 1.1	2.7 / 1.9 / .9				2.2 / 1.3 / 1.0	2.5 / 1.4 / .8
(9) Quick	1.3 / .4 / .2	1.5 / 1.1 / .3	1.6 / .6 / .3				1.3 / .7 / .4 (59)	1.5 / .8 / .4
(40)								

Note: the following is a rotated RMA financial ratio data table. Each cell contains three percentile values (upper / median / lower). Turnover rows show days and the turnover ratio.

Ratio					
10 Sales/Receivables	4 97.6 / 12 30.9 / 20 17.9	10 36.8 / 16 23.0 / 28 12.8	11 33.7 / 17 21.8 / 23 15.7	7 54.4 / 17 21.0 / 27 13.4	11 33.1 / 18 20.3 / 28 13.3
11 Cost of Sales/Inventory	13 28.8 / 35 10.4 / 88 4.1	28 13.1 / 46 8.0 / 66 5.5	27 7.4 / 71 5.2 / 83 4.4	23 15.9 / 45 8.1 / 82 4.5	27 13.7 / 42 8.7 / 75 4.9
12 Cost of Sales/Payables	23 15.9 / 43 8.4 / 72 5.1	18 20.2 / 33 10.9 / 48 7.6	27 13.6 / 35 10.3 / 70 5.2	21 17.7 / 28 13.0 / 48 7.6	16 23.3 / 31 11.7 / 66 5.6
Sales/Working Capital	16.1 / 284.0 / -14.9	8.3 / 13.2 / NM	8.9 / 11.8 / NM	11.4 / 24.3 / -397.8	8.6 / 34.2 / -66.3
13 EBIT/Interest	(33) 6.9 / 2.1 / .5	(15) 6.9 / 1.4 / -2.8	15.0 / 1.4 / -4.1	(60) 4.0 / 1.8 / .0	(51) 4.8 / 2.5 / .9
14 Net Profit + Depr., Dep., Amort./Cur. Mat. L./T/D			.7 / 1.1 / 2.8	(14) 3.5 / 1.6 / .4	(12) 3.8 / 1.9 / 1.1
15 Fixed/Worth	-.7 / -10.8 / -.8	(16) .4 / .7 / 2.6	(11) .7 / 1.1 / 2.8	(48) .4 / 1.3 / -11.4	(40) .5 / 1.4 / -2.2
16 Debt/Worth	2.5 / -36.4 / -3.0	.5 / 1.5 / 5.5	.5 / 1.5 / 3.3	.9 / 2.7 / -25.7	1.1 / 2.3 / -6.0
% Profit Before Taxes/Tangible Net Worth	(18) 97.9 / 18.1 / -1.0	(16) 36.0 / 12.7 / -8.1	(11) 26.1 / 6.2 / -28.6	(48) 31.7 / 9.8 / -2.8	(40) 49.0 / 10.5 / -.2
% Profit Before Taxes/Total Assets	27.2 / 6.5 / -.7	10.4 / 4.1 / -4.0	11.6 / 1.6 / -10.7	13.4 / 2.7 / -3.2	14.4 / 2.5 / -1.1
Sales/Net Fixed Assets	23.5 / 13.3 / 9.2	21.1 / 8.4 / 2.8	7.0 / 6.3 / 4.0	23.5 / 12.7 / 7.4	31.2 / 13.3 / 7.1
Sales/Total Assets	6.2 / 4.5 / 2.8	4.8 / 2.0 / 1.7	2.9 / 2.3 / 1.7	4.8 / 3.6 / 2.5	5.3 / 3.5 / 2.2
% Depr., Dep., Amort./Sales	(35) 1.2 / 2.0 / 3.0	(17) 1.3 / 2.6 / 3.2	1.8 / 3.9 / 4.4	(61) 1.1 / 2.0 / 3.1	(56) 1.0 / 1.7 / 2.8
% Officers', Directors', Owners' Comp/Sales	(26) 4.4 / 7.8 / 12.6			(37) 3.6 / 6.7 / 9.6	(38) 3.1 / 5.6 / 7.7
Net Sales ($)	32581M	54210M	122321M	12019M → 1590441M	1895855M / 467708M
Total Assets ($)	8046M	18467M	52205M	10552M → 297530M	500708M / 235386M

M = $ thousand   MM = $ million

© RMA 2005

RETAIL—Florists   NAICS 453110   (SIC 5992)

	Comparative Historical Data			Current Data Sorted By Sales					
Type of Statement	4/1/02-3/31/03 ALL	4/1/03-3/31/04 ALL	4/1/04-3/31/05 ALL	27 (4/1-9/30/04) 47 (10/1/04-3/31/05)					
				0-1MM	1-3MM	3-5MM	5-10MM	10-25MM	25MM & OVER
Unqualified	1	3	1			1	1	1	
Reviewed	7	5	7		2	1	1		
Compiled	26	28	14	7	4	3	3	3	
Tax Returns	34	23	38	20	10	2	2	1	2
Other	12	13	14	4	5	1			
NUMBER OF STATEMENTS	75	72	74	31	21	8	7	5	2
	%	%	%	%	%	%	%	%	%
ASSETS									
❶ Cash & Equivalents	13.6	7.0	11.4	10.2	10.7				
Trade Receivables (net)	12.9	15.9	14.7	15.5	12.9				
Inventory	22.6	22.7	21.3	25.4	18.4				
All Other Current	2.3	2.0	1.9	1.0	1.9				
Total Current	51.4	47.7	49.3	52.0	43.9				
Fixed Assets (net)	36.7	37.7	36.4	33.0	41.1				
Intangibles (net)	6.7	5.4	6.0	4.7	7.9				
All Other Non-Current	5.2	9.3	8.3	10.3	7.1				
Total	100.0	100.0	100.0	100.0	100.0				
LIABILITIES									
❷ Notes Payable-Short Term	8.7	9.9	9.9	10.8	12.8				
Cur. Mat.-L/T/D	7.1	4.3	10.6	20.2	2.6				
Trade Payables	19.6	20.3	20.9	24.1	21.9				
Income Taxes Payable	.2	.1	.1	.1	.0				
❸ All Other Current	12.8	13.4	11.0	16.1	6.9				
Total Current	48.3	48.0	52.5	71.3	44.2				
Long-Term Debt	37.8	33.6	29.2	34.3	33.7				
Deferred Taxes	.1	.2	.1	.0	.4				
All Other Non-Current	5.8	2.6	11.9	10.0	21.9				
Net Worth	7.9	15.6	6.2	-15.6	-.2				
Total Liabilities & Net Worth	100.0	100.0	100.0	100.0	100.0				
INCOME DATA									
❹ Net Sales	100.0	100.0	100.0	100.0	100.0				
❺ Gross Profit	51.8	51.4	56.3	57.0	53.8				
Operating Expenses	50.9	49.9	54.9	55.5	51.8				
❻ Operating Profit	.9	1.5	1.4	1.5	2.1				
All Other Expenses (net)	.7	.6	.0	.0	-.1				
❼ Profit Before Taxes	.3	1.0	1.4	1.5	2.2				
RATIOS									
❽ Current	2.2	1.8	2.3	1.6	2.3				
	1.2	1.0	1.1	1.0	1.5				
	.7	.6	.6	(30) .4	.6				
❾ Quick	1.2	1.1	1.4	.9	1.6				
	.6	(73) .4	.5	.4	.9				
	.3	.3	.3	.2	.3				

Ratio		(1)	(2)	(3)	(4)	(5)
Sales/Receivables (10)	UQ	4 / 102.3	9 / 39.7	6 / 62.4	4 / 96.8	5 / 67.9
	Med	14 / 25.7	15 / 23.9	14 / 26.0	15 / 24.2	12 / 30.3
	LQ	23 / 16.2	23 / 16.0	23 / 15.9	22 / 16.8	20 / 18.2
Cost of Sales/Inventory (11)	UQ	23 / 15.8	17 / 20.9	18 / 20.7	15 / 25.1	16 / 22.8
	Med	44 / 8.3	47 / 9.1	47 / 7.8	46 / 8.0	40 / 9.1
	LQ	83 / 4.4	77 / 4.7	81 / 4.5	91 / 4.0	79 / 4.6
Cost of Sales/Payables (12)	UQ	19 / 18.8	22 / 16.2	24 / 15.2	23 / 16.0	17 / 21.8
	Med	40 / 9.1	34 / 10.8	39 / 9.2	37 / 9.8	39 / 9.4
	LQ	61 / 6.0	62 / 5.9	62 / 5.9	69 / 5.3	59 / 6.2
Sales/Working Capital	UQ	10.7	14.4	10.7	18.3	9.5
	Med	45.4	UND	45.6	284.0	26.8
	LQ	-17.8	-16.5	-21.5	-14.9	-21.9
EBIT/Interest (13)		(69)	(61)	(63)	(26)	(16)
	UQ	5.9	8.2	6.9	6.3	6.9
	Med	2.4	1.7	1.5	1.5	2.4
	LQ	.4	-1.2	-1.4	.5	.4
Net Profit + Depr., Dep., Amort./Cur. Mat. L/T/D (14)		(11)		(11)		
	UQ	3.0		1.6		
	Med	2.3		.7		
	LQ	2.0		.2		
Fixed/Worth (15)	UQ	.6	.6	.6	.6	.6
	Med	3.3	1.7	1.7	9.0	1.7
	LQ	-1.4	-2.3	-2.5	-.8	-1.8
Debt/Worth (16)	UQ	1.2	1.2	.7	2.7	.6
	Med	5.5	5.9	4.0	107.0	5.3
	LQ	-3.4	-5.1	-5.3	-2.8	-3.3
% Profit Before Taxes/Tangible Net Worth		(47)	(47)	(48)	(16)	(12)
	UQ	55.6	57.6	44.7	52.2	34.5
	Med	12.9	12.7	9.6	8.1	16.3
	LQ	1.4	-13.0	-12.4	-6.7	.1
% Profit Before Taxes/Total Assets	UQ	14.2	14.0	16.1	17.8	15.0
	Med	4.7	3.6	3.7	5.4	5.7
	LQ	-3.1	-6.3	-4.0	-.7	-4.2
Sales/Net Fixed Assets	UQ	30.3	26.6	20.4	25.5	17.2
	Med	10.5	13.5	12.2	13.3	11.0
	LQ	4.4	4.4	5.6	6.9	4.1
Sales/Total Assets	UQ	4.8	4.9	5.0	5.9	5.2
	Med	3.1	3.2	3.4	3.8	3.5
	LQ	2.1	2.0	1.9	2.2	1.8
% Depr., Dep., Amort./Sales		(62)	(64)	(65)	(28)	(17)
	UQ	1.2	1.2	1.3	1.1	1.9
	Med	2.4	2.0	2.5	1.9	2.7
	LQ	4.2	3.4	3.9	2.8	3.4
% Officers', Directors', Owners' Comp/Sales		(47)	(36)	(40)	(21)	
	UQ	3.8	4.4	4.1	5.7	
	Med	5.6	6.0	6.8	10.0	
	LQ	9.5	10.0	10.8	13.9	

Net Sales ($): 2627300M, 2622449M, 1811572M, 17467M, 33783M, 33031M, 47787M, 89063M, 1590441M

Total Assets ($): 648150M, 990427M, 386800M, 5966M, 12551M, 18655M, 14443M, 37655M, 297530M

M = $ thousand   MM = $ million

PART III
PUTTING
IT INTO
ACTION

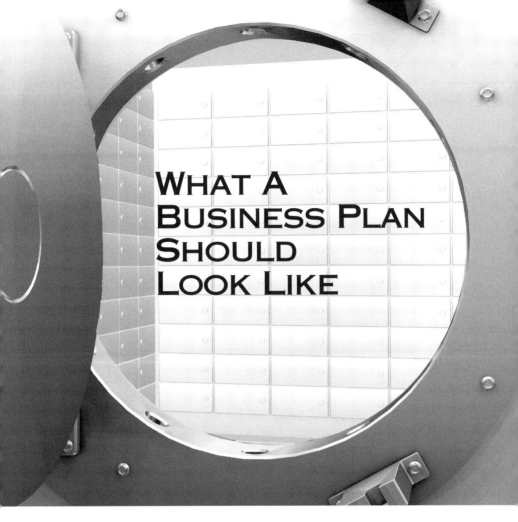

WHAT A BUSINESS PLAN SHOULD LOOK LIKE

Congratulations! Now that you've thoroughly considered the Ten Action Steps leading to the creation of your company, you're ready to write your plan. Remember that your business plan represents who you are. You want it to be professional, organized, and persuasive. It should demonstrate how completely you have researched your business concept and your commitment to seeing the project through to a successful completion.

The first physical impression your plan makes when it arrives on a reader's desk is crucial. If it has been folded into a thin paper envelope, it will arrive dog-eared and creased. If you've used a paper clip to hold it together, the sheets will separate as soon as the reader tries to flip through the pages. If you've used flimsy paper, your plan will look old and worn out by the time it's passed along to the next reader.

To help you understand the importance of the physical presentation of your business plan, let's examine exactly how it should look.

The Physical Qualities

The look of your business plan will create an indelible first impression—negative or positive. I'm shocked to see how often my clients at the Field Center make the mistake of creating a presentation that overshadows the content of the plan. Many entrepreneurs commit a great deal of effort and expense to designing an eye-catching written presentation. I've seen several that were true works of art—slickly produced with fanciful graphics and expensive, glossy paper. Other clients have cobbled together a sloppy business plan mixed with both original and photocopied pages generated by different computers and printed in mismatching fonts.

In all of these cases, even the most persuasive text was completely eclipsed by the physical presentation. Such artfully or poorly produced business plans give the impression that these entrepreneurs either have more flash than polish or are too disorganized and incompetent to start their own businesses. The physical qualities of your plan should demonstrate that you took exceptional care to produce it and that you are a competent, meticulous, enthusiastic, and knowledgeable professional.

Neatness counts

If your business plan represents you, think about the impression you would make entering a potential investor's office with your shoelace flopping and your tie splattered with the pea soup you had for lunch, or with your slip showing and your silk blouse missing a beautifully embossed button. A disheveled appearance sends an instantly negative, and often unalterable, message about you to the other person. So does a messy business plan.

I have seen plans that looked as if they had been pecked out on 1937 Underwood typewriters by major holders of White-Out stock. I once reviewed a plan for a financial consulting venture in which words in the typed text were crossed out, with handwritten changes squeezed between the single spaced lines. The columns of numbers in the fiscal sections weren't lined up properly, so the subtotals and totals weren't clear. The content of the plan was actually rather impressive, but as I thumbed through the messy, amateurish pages, all I could think was, "What kind of product or service will these people be able to produce for their customers?"

One of my clients submitted a meticulous and persuasive plan, but left off a contact name, address, and telephone number. Another failed to include a heading with the name of her company and page numbers on each sheet. Both omissions could spell disaster if the order of the pages became jumbled, or the investors wanted to call to arrange a meeting.

Speaking of spelling disaster, misspellings, incorrect financial numbers, inconsistent text fonts, or pages that fall out easily, all reflect badly on you. Your plan must be neat, accurate, well proofread, and generated on a computer, so that changes and updates can be made easily. If you know how to use a spreadsheet program, do so, but a clean, clear list of financial figures produced on a quality printer will work well, too.

Color printing is nice, but not essential. Have your plan spiral-bound at your local copy store, with a clear top sheet and an opaque back sheet to further protect it during what you hope will be extensive reading and handling. Spiral binding also keeps the pages in order and allows your plan to be opened flat for easy reading. With a neat, accurate presentation, you will greatly increase your chances of convincing investors not only to read about your potential business, but to support it as well.

Decent paper is proper

Be sure the quality of paper you choose for printing is good enough so it stands up to multiple readings, but not too contrived or elaborate that you actually send the wrong message to your investors. I once saw a plan for a Christmas tree ornament store printed on alternating red and green paper. Not only was this idea precious, it also rendered the text extremely difficult to read.

Another client presented a business plan to me that was done entirely on glossy card stock. This, too, was hard to read under any artificial lighting conditions and made flipping back and forth between the pages virtually impossible. Using stock that is difficult to read, or inordinately expensive, may indicate that you're not very serious about your business plan or that you're a spendthrift who enjoys squandering money. Needless to say, none of these qualities will encourage potential investors to support your endeavor. Standard 24 lb. paper, commonly used in a laser printers, is the best choice.

Excessive length equals long-windedness

Coming to the point quickly and effectively is important in both speaking and writing. Do not be fooled into believing that the longer and more detailed your plan, the more impressive it will appear to potential investors. Being excessively wordy implies that you do not value the small amount of precious time readers have to evaluate your written business plan. Take a look at the four sentence executive summary for Bug-Be-Gone on page 163. Four sentences should not necessarily be your goal, but if you strive for a statement this distilled, you should be able to cover all ten action steps with very few words.

The same is true for the text of your business plan. Although this section should detail each of the ten action steps, you want to keep your statements clear, pithy, and highly readable. William Strunk, Jr. and E.B. White, in their famous 1,300 word book *The Elements of Style*, emphasize rule 13: "Omit needless words." As the authors explain, "This requires not that the writer make all his sentences short, or that he avoid all detail, but that every word tell." Chances are your first business plan draft will have many needless words. Find them and eliminate them.

Additional media is not a must

In this era of Palm Pilots, PowerPoint projections, and other innovative communication techniques, it's tempting to employ cutting-edge technology in presenting your business plan. Some technology can be eye-catching and make a memorable impression, but it should only supplement your written plan, not replace it or overshadow it. In fact, many of those who read your plan will never meet you, see an in-person presentation, or look at supplemental material such as videos or DVDs. They will base their decision solely on the written plan, which must achieve your purpose on its own.

I once saw a plan for a commercial fishing venture that was presented as a slick videotape showing boats, large catches of fish, and happy consumers enjoying elaborate seafood dinners. It was quite impressive, but I suppose the authors of this plan thought it too mundane to include a few pieces of paper outlining their capabilities or projected returns to their potential investors.

The Actual Layout

Banks, loan institutions and professional investors review dozens of business plans every day. They want to grasp the business concept easily and evaluate the numbers quickly. To make sure their staff time is spent effectively, most financial institutions and investors prefer that all business plans conform to a particular format. Although there may be individual variations from one firm to another, which you must determine in advance, most formats are fairly standard and include the following five components in this order:

- **A cover page** that is cleanly designed and contains all the right information.
- **A table of contents** that is short and to the point.
- **An executive summary** that is concise, but touches on all Ten Action Steps in one paragraph.

- **A complete text** that is well edited and describes the ten action steps in detail.
- **An appendix** with a complete set of exhibits.

When your business plan is complete, have it spiral bound with firm plastic backing and a clear protective cover sheet.

The cover page is the first impression of your business plan. The cover page must be neat and legible, and contain all the basic information so reviewers can contact you quickly and easily—that is, if they want to schedule an in-person meeting. Readers don't want to thumb through the entire plan to find your name, the title of your company, or its purpose.

The cover page should display the following:

- **The name of your company** in large type near the top of the page.
- **A single phrase** describing what your company does, directly beneath the company name.
- **The names of the founder or partners** involved, half-way down the page.
- **The name of the primary contact person**, near the bottom of the page.
- **The contact information for reaching this person**, including telephone number, fax number, e-mail address, and mailing address, directly beneath the contact person's name.

The following page is an example of a clear, clean cover page.

Bug-Be-Gone

A Company that Manufactures
Nontoxic, Fruit-scented Bug Spray

Roger Roach
Founder and Chief Executive Officer

Contact: Roger Roach

Telephone: (888) BUG-BGONE or (212) 284-2343

Fax: (212) 284-2344

Website: www.bug-be-gone.com

E-mail: rroach@bug-be-gone.com

Mailing Address:

Roger Roach, C.E.O.
Bug-Be-Gone, Inc.
123 Silverfish Lane
Infested, Indiana 65123

Date: April 2008

The table of contents is helpful, even if your plan is fairly brief, and necessary if your plan is still lengthy after numerous edits. Place the table of contents directly after the cover page, so investors can turn to any specific section quickly. You may also consider attaching identifying tabs to each of the sections, so readers can locate them more readily.

The executive summary is ideally a one page (or shorter!) overview of your plan, with a compelling argument for the success of your business concept. More than a simple explanation of your idea, the executive summary is the hook that must grab and hold the attention of the funding sources evaluating your plan. If potential investors don't like what they see in the executive summary, they rarely read any further, and your beautifully crafted plan will be tossed onto the already sky-high reject pile.

Most bankers and venture capital firms see hundreds of plans every year. If your executive summary doesn't immediately assert that your plan merits attention, you're history.

An executive summary should briefly cover the Ten Essential Action Steps outlined in Part II, which are:

1. **Define Your Company:** *What Will You Accomplish For Others...and Yourself?*

2. **Identify Your Company's Needs:** *What Will You Require To Get Started?*

3. **Choose A Winning Strategy:** *What Will Distinguish Your Product or Service from Your Competition?*

4. **Analyze Your Market:** *Who Will Want Your Product or Service?*

5. **Develop A Strong Marketing Campaign:** *How Will You Reach Your Customers and What Will You Say To Them?*

6. **Build A Dynamic Sales Effort:** *How Will You Attract Customers?*

7. **Design Your Company:** *How Will You Hire and Organize Your Work Force?*

8. **Target Your Funding Sources:** *Where Will You Find Your Financing?*

9. **Explain Your Financial Data:** *How Will You Convince Others To Invest In Your Endeavor?*

10. **Use The RMA Database:** *Check Your Answers Against the Answer Key.*

The following executive summary for the Bug-Be-Gone Corporation is only four sentences long, but it mentions all ten action steps clearly and succinctly:

> Bug-Be-Gone Corporation is seeking to raise $10 million in equity capital from individuals who will invest at least $1 million each (2, 8) to develop and market a unique line of fruit-scented insecticides that are nontoxic to humans and pets (1, 3, 4, 5). Bug-Be-Gone is owned and managed by Roger Roach, whose 20 years of experience in the insect extermination business will enable him to hire the most knowledgeable entomologists and the most precise bug sprayers in the industry (7). The company has already received preliminary orders from the three major firms that supply 80 percent of the California market, which consumes 50 percent of all insecticides in the United States (4, 5, 6). The financial projections show the company achieving higher than average profit margins (10) and that equity investors will receive returns in excess of 35 percent annually by the third year of operation (1, 9).

If your venture is more complex than Bug-Be-Gone's, you may need two or three paragraphs, but polish and trim until you have the most highly distilled executive summary possible.

Here are a few more examples:

Sunny City Budget Motel

There is no budget hotel within the Sunny City market. Relative to standard measures of hotel/motel rooms, for the volume of travelers on the adjacent interstate highway, the city population, and jobs in the market, the Sunny City hotel/motel market is under built and represents an opportunity for new hotels and motels.

I have identified a location adjacent to the interstate highway, within two miles of downtown, that can be purchased for the construction of a hotel or motel. The XYZ national budget hotel chain is willing to sell a franchise for this location. The cost numbers for the land and construction are below the franchisor's national averages, while room rates are projected to be at or above their figures. Financial projections show that $2 million in equity investment will earn 21 percent returns, and $8 million in debt can be repaid in eight years.

The LawnRider Company

The riding lawn mower industry has grown threefold in the last 15 years. The trends show the market is very sensitive to price and features. The LawnRider Company is being formed to become a major player in this market. A line of LawnRiders has been designed that adds features to mid-priced riding lawn mowers previously seen only in high-end machines. LawnRider has negotiated a contract with a Korean factory to manufacture the machines and give LawnRider the low cost advantage in this market. The largest home-center company in the U.S. market has agreed to carry LawnRider exclusively in its 1,200 stores. Both agreements are negotiated. The key remaining elements for LawnRider's success is for the company to market the product. Towards that end, a detailed marketing plan has been created. LawnRider is seeking $4 million in investment, which is projected to earn 32 percent average annual return over the next three years.

Mom's Restaurant

Mom's has been a successful restaurant with more than $2.5 million in annual revenue, and profits of more than $80,000 annually for the last nine years. The building, land, and contents are appraised at $425,000. Janet Wise, the founder and manager of Mom's, is looking to sell. My Restaurant Corp. is a company managed by Bob Wyler, who has been the head chef at Mom's for six years, and his wife Sylvia Wyler, who has been a manager at Mom's for four years. My Restaurant has negotiated the purchase of Mom's Restaurant, including the land on which the restaurant and parking lot stand, for $350,000.

The Wylers are investing $100,000 and are looking to obtain a bank loan for the balance of $250,000 to be secured by an SBA guarantee, the building, and the land. The restaurant performs within industry standards as reflected in the RMA data for restaurants. The Wylers have an excellent personal credit record. There are no outstanding claims or liabilities against Mom's. The economy of the neighborhood, based on employment, housing prices, and new construction, is strong.

These are four compelling business plan summaries. When you write your executive summary, keep in mind that it, like your entire plan, is a document with a purpose. The Sunny City plan is written for investors and lenders; the LawnRider for investors; and the Mom's Restaurant plan for a bank. Ask yourself what is missing from your plan or research that could keep your plan from accomplishing its purpose. If you find nothing, then you are ready to put the entire plan together.

The text presents a more detailed version of the Ten Action Steps. Remember to check these points in designing the layout of the text:

Don't forget to paginate and put a heading on *each* page of your plan so that if the pages get separated from each other, your readers can reconstruct your plan.

Design your text with boldface, underlining, and enough white space to make the different subjects and paragraphs stand out visually. This will enable your readers to find particular points more readily.

Double check your table of contents against the text to make certain you have included all the right headings and subheadings. It's astonishing how many business plan writers forget to compare the table of contents to the actual contents!

Use crisp, clear language. A business plan is not the place to impress people with your extensive knowledge of your industry's arcane jargon. If you write in this style, a potential investor may believe that you're not capable of explaining your plan clearly. You may be perceived as a person who is unable to work well with employees or suppliers who might not speak your lingo.

Include a time line, which helps show your prospective investors when you expect to accomplish key milestones. This is discussed in greater detail in Part III: How To Create A Time Line beginning on page 169.

The appendix of exhibits should consist of detailed information that would break up the flow of the text, such as market studies or copies of your partners' résumés, or data you may wish to be kept confidential, such as partnership agreements. Interleaving these documents into the actual text of your business plan will only slow the reader down. It's better to footnote the text with a phrase such as "detailed market studies are available on request," or "see appendix for partners' résumés."

If you have information that you will be giving only to certain readers, it's important to bind your appendix of exhibits separately from the main body of your text, so that you can provide it on an as-needed basis to your readers. The cover page of the appendix should mirror the cover page of the plan with the word *Appendix* clearly displayed.

Remember that all tables and exhibits must be completely self-explanatory. You must spell out what the information is, where it comes from, and any underlying assumptions you have made in projections. Think about people reading your plan on an airplane or in the middle of the night. They can't reach you to ask their questions, so the plan needs to supply all the answers.

Have Outsiders Read It

When you have finished writing your plan, ask friends or colleagues with business experience to read it and offer brutally honest comments about its clarity and persuasiveness. You may eventually want to follow their advice about tearing down the restaurant you want to buy and putting up a car wash in its place, but at this point, you primarily need to know if your plan is clear and complete.

Make The Time To Give It A Rest

It's extremely helpful to put your business plan in a drawer for any period of time you can afford before you reread it. This bit of perspective can reveal flaws or weaknesses that you hadn't initially noticed.

How Long Should It Be?

Many of my Field Center clients have asked me how long it should take to write a plan and how many pages a plan should be. It's a little like Abraham Lincoln's response to the person who needled him about his own excessive height. "How long should a man's legs be?" he was asked. He answered, "Long enough to reach the ground."

I have seen persuasive and thorough plans that were only five pages long, and equally strong plans that exceeded 100 pages. Most plans require about 20 to 30 pages to cover the Ten Action Steps, including appendices and financial projections, but a plan needs only to be long enough to convince potential funders that they should invest in your endeavor.

How Long Should It Take Me?

Most entrepreneurs work on their plans from initial concept to polished final version over a period of several weeks. It's rare for someone to research and write a quality plan in less than a week, unless most of the background work and financial projections have already been done. However, after I've watched people work on plans for months, I begin to think that they would rather write plans than start a business. At the other extreme are the equally unconvincing clients who download a plan from a website and run a few find-and-replace functions to insert their names and the names of their businesses in place of those in the sample plan. Would you want to invest your money with a person who put so little time and effort into a business plan?

If you aim for a 20 to 30-page document, and budget a few weeks' time, you will be in the average range of most of my clients.

Reread And Revise

A final polish is always worth the effort.

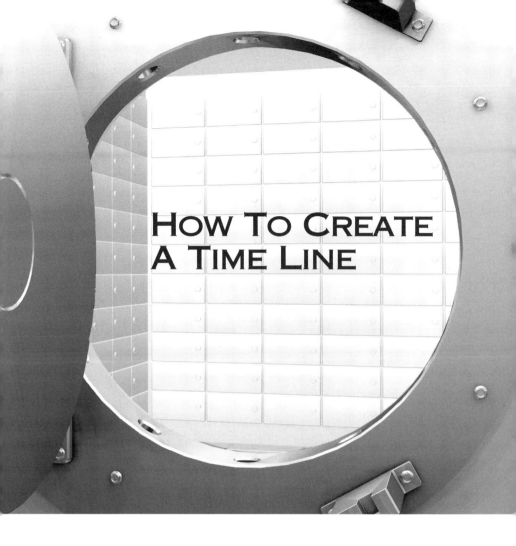

How To Create A Time Line

A time line is an extremely useful tool in designing and presenting your business plan. Depending on the complexity of your plan, your time line could be a simple list of the key dates of expected events arranged in chronological order. If you're planning a restaurant, a time line will estimate when you expect to rent your store front, begin your renovations, order your tables and chairs, hire your cook and waitresses, and open your doors for business. If your venture is very complicated, such as a business that manufactures major appliances or develops complex software, your time line may list thousands of steps, all linked in a sophisticated computer program.

The Primary Components

A time line will force you to allot a length of time for each step in your business plan. Here are the primary components of a time line:

Develop a realistic schedule

You need to give your potential investors and lenders a reasonably accurate estimate of how long it will take you to establish your business, and make it profitable. I have advised many entrepreneurs who tend to gloss over these details in what I call the *build-it-and-they-will-come phenomenon*. It may be true that customers will come when you're open for business, but getting to that point may involve many time-consuming steps, such as obtaining zoning approvals, licenses, and financing. Unless you'll be working from a corner of your living room, opening an office requires, at a minimum, negotiating a lease, ordering and delivering furniture, and having phones installed.

Create an accurate budget

The process of creating the time line will help you produce a detailed and accurate budget. Since budgets and financial projections all have time dimensions, a time line will indicate when items need to be ordered, employees hired, and fees paid. On the revenue side, the time line can indicate when you estimate receiving any outside funding, and when you will begin to turn a profit. It will also be helpful to establish the extent of the initial profit and when you expect it to increase in the future.

Focus on the critical path

In any project that has many steps, such as starting a business or even writing a business plan, there is a *critical path* of events that will determine whether you complete your project on time. The examples that follow demonstrate the critical path for a business that sells cotton candy at a fair. Any delay in completing tasks along the critical path delays the completion of the entire project. Delays in tasks that are not on the critical path can be tolerated, because they will *not* delay completion of the entire project. Therefore, you should focus on those events that comprise this critical path, and work hard to make sure they stay on schedule.

Establish a system of accountability

Once you have created your time line, you have benchmarks against which to compare your actual operation and performance. The time line will keep you constantly apprised of what you need to focus on next, or what steps might be holding up your progress. No business creation follows its plan precisely. With a time line in place, you can easily check your progress, and revise your plans as needed.

Demonstrate your professionalism

A bankable business plan must demonstrate your qualifications and professionalism. Providing a detailed and realistic time line clearly shows potential investors and lenders that you know how to build your business, that you are reasonably optimistic about your venture, and that you have projected far enough into the future to accurately assess both your business needs and goals.

Give feedback to your investors

Just as the time line works for you as a planning tool, it will work for your investors in judging your performance. You will be asked many times, "How are you doing compared to your plan?" The time line gives you a simple, presentable method to show your investors, bankers, employees, and suppliers precisely how well you are doing compared to your written plan.

Examples Of Time Lines

The simplest time line is a list of activities along with their projected dates and key expenditures. Here is a time line for an entrepreneur who wants to set up a business selling cotton candy at the county fair. Because a delay in any step can slow the entire project, each activity is part of the critical path.

Activity	Dates	Expenditures Required
File with Fair Manager to get permit/location	October 23	$50 fee required
Obtain permit	December 15	—
Order trailer and cotton candy maker	December 16	$3,000 deposit required
Delivery of trailer and cotton candy maker	March 1	$5,000 payment required
Take trailer for painting	March 10	$750 deposit required
Pick up painted trailer	March 22	$2,000 payment required
Order candy-making supplies	April 20	$600 payment required
Supplies delivered	May 1	—
Test weekend at Little League games	May 15-17	$300 for employees
Set up at County Fair	June 3	—
Fair week	June 6-13	$1,200 for employees

Gantt Charts

Gantt charts (named for their developer, Henry Gantt) are similar to the cotton candy business time line, but with a graphic presentation of each activity. The major advantage of the Gantt chart is that it is easy to see whether the various activities listed are running sequentially, parallel to each other, or overlap. Gantt charts can be created using word-processing programs, spreadsheet programs, such as Lotus or Excel, or specialized programs, such as Microsoft Project.

Gantt charts offer several advantages over a list format:

- You can fill in or color over the lines that represent each task as the task is completed.

- You can draw a line across all the branches of the chart to see how many tasks are running longer than projected.

- You can create sub task lists that show all the underlying components of any single task on the chart. This can happen automatically if you use project management software.

Gantt Chart for Opening a Florist Shop

Activities	Jan	Feb	Mar	Apr	May	Jun
Write Plan		███	███			
Search for Location		███	███			
Obtain Financing			███	███		
Renovate Shop				███		
Development of Major Accounts			███	███	███	███
Search for and Sign up Suppliers		███	███	███	███	
Grand Opening					███	

PERT Charts

The most sophisticated time line system is the **Program Evaluation** and **Review Technique**, or **PERT** chart. PERT charts make it possible to determine the critical path of a project, which is the precise sequence of activities that must be completed on time in order to avoid delays. PERT charts are most useful for projects that are highly complex with many interdependent steps, or where the cost of delay can be crippling. Large-scale construction projects, for example, often use PERT charts.

Similar to the simple time line, or Gantt chart, a PERT chart is produced by creating a list of all the activities that must be accomplished to bring your plan to fruition, along with an estimate of how long that process will take. For each activity on the time line, you should also list its immediate prerequisites. For example, you can't sign the contract to construct the factory until the bank loan is approved and the zoning variances are granted. Once you have listed all the activities and their immediate prerequisites, you can create a time line similar to the PERT example.

To determine which activities are on the critical path, you can look backward from completion to find the shortest route. You can also follow a procedure outlined in the reference material and estimate the earliest and latest completion times for each activity and then find the shortest route. For complex projects, you can also employ software that does this calculation automatically along with charting and updating.

I believe that your basic time line should include no more than twenty activities. Over twenty and it will be hard to fit the time line on one page and you're better off using a software package such as Microsoft Project.

The following page has an example of a PERT chart.

PERT Chart

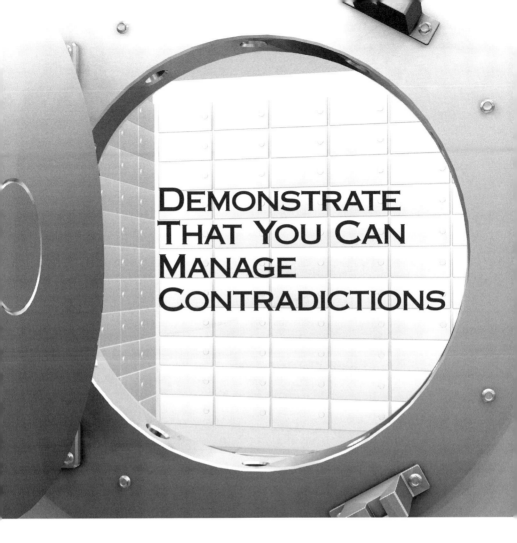

DEMONSTRATE THAT YOU CAN MANAGE CONTRADICTIONS

There are inherent contradictions that you should take into consideration when writing your business plan. They involve your strategy, your view of your competition, your vision, and your presentation. Most entrepreneurs I advise struggle with these contradictions; however if you identify them in advance and learn how to manage them, they will not undermine your business plan.

The four main contradictions to keep in mind as you prepare your business plan are:

Keep It Simple . . . Yet Detailed

Your plan needs to make a simple, compelling case as to why

your business concept represents a strong investment opportunity. Most funders want to see the detail behind your conclusions, such as financial figures, analysis of your competition, lists of potential customers, and market research. Your task in writing the plan is to give everyone the specific information they demand without burying the clear and simple message of why your business idea is a smart investment.

Remember that a business plan is a document written for a purpose. Most often, that purpose is to convince people to contribute resources to your venture. You must answer all readers' particular questions to their complete satisfaction. Issues that are important to some readers will be irrelevant to others. Your dilemma is to give all the answers to all the questions without losing your readers in a morass of detail.

Don't despair! You can resolve this contradiction and create an extremely well-organized, balanced business plan by employing three basic tools: a complete table of contents, eye-catching headings, and a clearly labeled appendix of exhibits. This allows readers to locate the topics that are important to them while skipping over the less relevant sections.

A table of contents serves the purpose of giving your reader an overview of your plan and help in finding topics. For example, a potential investor will probably want to study your projected returns in detail. The table of contents will guide this reader to the section on financial projections, with a subheading for projected returns. This particular section, however, will be less important to future suppliers, who will be more eager to read about your market and sales projections.

Headings should appear every time you change the subject and should be complete enough to clarify what topic is covered in each section. I have seen plans that are solid blocks of type, rather like densely written college papers. Faced with this format, the investor must either commit to reading every word, or risk missing parts that she believes are important. I have tried to use headings in this book to help you locate subjects of importance to you and sincerely hope I have succeeded!

An **appendix** is a section of specific documents bound separately from your written business plan. It supplies information too detailed or specialized to be included in the body of the text, such as lists of potential customers, copies of materials from your competitors, industry reports, or the résumés of your company principals. I have seen plans that place the financial projections in the appendix, but this sends the wrong message to readers who may assume that profits are not central to the plan, when they *always* are.

Employing these tools will help you create a plan that is focused and simple, yet complete and easy for readers to follow and analyze. You will show that profits are important, that you are a thorough researcher, and that you can address every reader's issues.

Striking a balance in your written plan between stating a simple goal and providing complete information will also demonstrate that you'll be a flexible manager who can focus on the details while still maintaining the course toward your company's overall objectives. After reading your plan, people will see that you are honest and qualified.

Focus On Growth . . . Even In Mature Industries

Investors generally prefer to see business plans for companies with high growth potential. Growth of revenue usually translates into increased profits and business value. This growth fuels returns for investors, generates more cash to pay interest, and creates new opportunities for employees, suppliers, and business partners. As an entrepreneur, you should also prefer to plan for business growth, because any increased profits and business value directly accrue to your benefit. You have probably witnessed growth opportunities in your industry since you first hatched your idea, such as an overlooked consumer group, a better product that will attract more customers, or a rapidly growing market.

If your business is in an industry that is experiencing high growth, most investors will assume that your company will grow right along with this rapidly expanding field. This is not always the case, because certain fast-growing industries, such as e-commerce, attracted investors faster than they attracted new customers. The Internet and e-commerce businesses that succeeded over the last decade are exceptions. The reality is that the vast majority of industries grow at the same modest pace of the overall economy, which is about 2 to 3 percent per year.

The contradiction here is this: everyone wants to see dynamic growth projections in your business plan, but most industries are growing slowly. You cannot resolve these two seemingly contradictory statements, but you can make this conflict work to strengthen your written plan by doing the following:

- **Acknowledge** the contradiction.

- **Explain the benefits**, such as stability and fewer new competitors, of owning a business in this slow-growing industry now.

- **Present** opportunities in this industry, such as being able to purchase competitors at low prices, and propose doing so if it fits your plan.

- **Offer a strategy** that takes customers away from existing competitors rather than simply capturing a share of new customers.

- **Detail your operations** to explain how you will attract and retain these customers.

I have seen many plans for mature industries that have very ambitious growth objectives. Most plans fail to explain how this growth will be achieved. Others simply state that their management is so superior to their competitors' teams that they will far exceed industry expectations and standards. That simply doesn't work, and it's usually simply wrong. Strong management is essential for successful ventures, but bankers, investors, and partners want to know *specifically* what management will do to create growth. If you discuss your business benefits, opportunities, strategies, and operations in detail, you will be able to demonstrate strong growth potential even in a slow-growing mature industry.

Reassure Investors...Even With Competition All Around

Here is an executive summary for a business that will *definitely* reassure investors:

> I have obtained, at no cost, the exclusive license to collect tolls on the Golden Gate Bridge. The California Bridge Authority will continue to maintain the bridge at taxpayer expense. I need to raise $10,000 for the purchase of bags to carry the money to the bank. For every $1,000 invested, investors can expect to receive 1 percent of future profits, or about $1 million per year.

If only it were so easy! Since the demise of colonial rule, America hasn't seen such good deals. Just think for a minute about what makes this deal so reassuring to investors: you have no competitors. Aside from a few ferries or the alternative of a 50-mile drive, there is no other way to get from San Francisco to Marin County. There is no competition nor is there any prospect of new competitors.

Many bankers and investors—often without coming out and saying it—are looking for competition-free businesses, such as the exclusive Golden Gate Bridge franchise. Here are examples of the excuses investors may use to avoid supporting a non-exclusive business:

- There is too much competition in your industry for us to feel comfortable. Just opening the *Yellow Pages* under your business category and seeing so many competitors scares us away from this industry.

- What's to keep a copycat business from opening up next door to you?

- The barriers to entry are just too low for us.

The fact is that virtually *every* business has competition. The point of your business plan is to analyze the market, the competition, and your company's position, not to try fruitlessly to find a business that has no competition. Your business plan must make clear that you, like all entrepreneurs, function in a competitive market and will succeed by identifying and serving your customers while managing your business profitably. By focusing your business plan on these issues, you will address the conflict about competition head on, and weaken its potential to derail your goal of gaining the support you need to start your venture.

Commit To Your Plan...But Be Willing To Pursue Other Good Opportunities

Many investors believe that for a business to be successful it needs a driving force or visionary who is committed to winning at any cost. They want to see a *Knight in Shining Armor* who will fight any foe to bring the plan to fruition. Many investors screen business plans looking for this brand of unwavering leadership and, to some extent, they're right.

There are limits to this ideal which can create yet another baffling contradiction. The business plan you write, and are committed to now, may require adjustment in the future. Market conditions, competition, economic factors, and technology—just to name a few issues—can change drastically and will force your plan to change as well. Those movie studios that remained committed to producing silent movies after talkies were invented, were soon silenced forever by bankruptcy. Electronics manufacturers who were slow to adopt the transistors that replaced vacuum tubes were soon expiring in an economic vacuum.

Your plan should present you as both committed and highly motivated, but also capable of looking for new opportunities and better ways to operate your business. Investors need reassurance that once you attain your goal, like the entrepreneur who hoped to find a cure for feather loss in parakeets, you will remain determined to make your venture profitable. People who start businesses with personal agendas, such as getting revenge on a former employer or finding a cure for a disease that afflicts someone they love, often meet resistance from investors.

To resolve this contradiction, I suggest that you include a section in the plan that speculates about some of the directions in which you may want the business to go in the long term. For example, you can discuss changes in technology that you might adopt in the future to improve service, reduce costs, or expand your market. A plan for the Squid Pancake Restaurant could discuss possible developments in the squid-farming industry and the opportunities they present, such as expanding your menu to include all-you-can-eat squid dinners, or adding chicken dishes if squid proves to be less popular than anticipated.

Your plan should demonstrate how well you're attuned to the market and its shifts and how willing you are to make adaptive changes, while still believing that your concept is the best possible course for today's conditions.

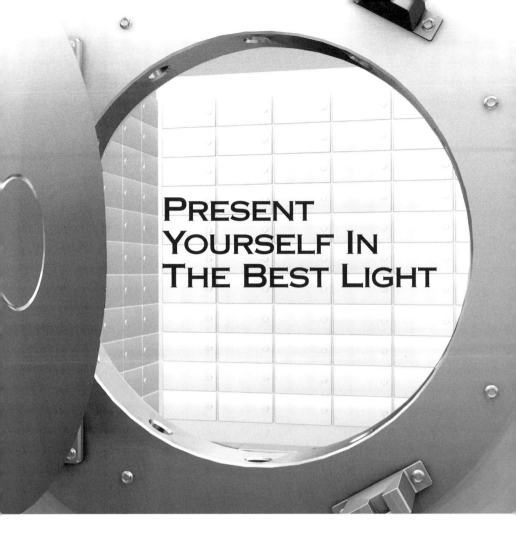

PRESENT YOURSELF IN THE BEST LIGHT

The talents, experience, and enthusiasm you bring to your enterprise are unique. They provide some of the most compelling reasons for others to finance your concept. Keep in mind that investors invest in people more than ideas. Even if your potential business has many competitors, or is not on the cutting edge of an industry, the qualifications and commitment you demonstrate in your plan can convince others to proffer their support.

Your résumé will be included in the separate appendix of exhibits, so the text of your business plan is not the place to list every job you've ever had. It *is* the place to emphasize qualifying skills that may not be readily apparent from your résumé. Convincing potential funders that you are highly qualified to establish and run your venture is critical.

Say you are the Field Center client who wants to open the restaurant featuring squid-flavored pancakes. Investors won't be initially impressed by your long and successful career as a commercial airline pilot. They may be much more swayed by the fact that from the age of eight to eighteen, you worked after school and weekends in your father's delicatessen. This information has probably never appeared on your professional résumé, which stresses the number of flying hours you have logged, your outstanding safety record, and the citations you received for the most on-time flights. Working for so long and intimately in a family-owned retail food business indicates that you know how to supervise cooks, run a cash register, and order perishable foodstuffs in bulk. You are probably even an expert in the Heimlich maneuver which, with squid-flavored pancakes, may come in handy.

Perhaps before you embarked on your flying career, you joined the Peace Corps and worked in a country that happened to be the world's largest squid harvester. The knowledge you've acquired about the squid business and the contacts you have maintained in your Peace Corps country will enable you to purchase tons of high-quality squid more cheaply and rapidly than any of your competitors.

Don't overlook the impact being a pilot may have on your ability to run a restaurant, especially if those skills are not apparent to your potential investors. You should stress that you know how to supervise a crew of people working together to make a group experience, if not comfortable, at least safe. You have undoubtedly handled dissatisfied or enraged customers. Even that B.A. in art history may enable you to teach cooks how to make their dishes more appealing to the eye.

If you have partners or staff, you must cover the same issues for them, especially if they bring skills to the venture you don't have. Perhaps one is an expert in state-of-the-art handheld computers that waiters can use to send orders immediately to the kitchen or to tally bills or approve credit card purchases within seconds. Another may be a champion napkin folder who can create caricatures of customers as soon as they sit down at their tables.

Your unique qualifications will separate you from all the other people who have sought venture capital for squid-flavored pancake restaurants. Boasting about these skills is not hubris; it indicates that you have highly-honed business savvy.

The body of your text and your attached résumé must state who you are, what you have done, what you can do and what you will do. Think of these elements of your business plan as a personal sales pitch about your qualifications to start your business and guide it to success.

You should demonstrate that *you* are as bankable as your business plan. Your qualifications assure financial supporters that your goals are reasonable and attainable. They are just as important as developing the right marketing strategy or establishing your competitive advantage, because *you* must implement these ideas and make them profitable. Prices don't select themselves, and customer service doesn't evolve without strong leadership from an exacting manager. Your marketing strategy, competitive advantage, and sales efforts are useless without you and your qualifications.

Stressing your enthusiasm is not the most effective way to indicate to potential investors and lenders that you have the skills, savvy and determination to be successful. Focus on your accomplishments and experience that apply to starting and running your company. You must also convince funders that your partners or the employees you are planning to hire for their particular experience or skills are equally qualified.

The text of your business plan that stresses your credentials has the same purpose as the résumé you attach to your appendix, but each is achieved through quite different means. A résumé should be short and easy to read, so potential supporters can see a quick overview of the experience, training, and education you bring to your venture. The text is where you can elaborate on the skills you brought to each of your previous positions and the areas of expertise that you developed on each job. The résumé provides the bare bones of your experience; the text supplies the muscle. Both need to be strong.

Let's take a more detailed look at how the text of the plan and your résumé can help create a convincing case that you are the best person to start and run your business.

The Text Of Your Business Plan

The body of your business plan is where you can elaborate on talents and skills that are not obvious from the work record listed on your résumé. Remember the earlier example of the commercial airline pilot who wanted to open the restaurant featuring squid-flavored pancakes? His résumé will show that he enlisted in the Peace Corps, but it will not indicate that the country he served in is the largest harvester of squid in the world or that the contacts he made there will enable him to buy and export squid efficiently.

His résumé will mention his professional citations for the best safety and on-time records, which indicate that he is goal oriented and takes pride in the service he provides his customers. Only in the text can he explain how having been a pilot will enable him to train his staff to maintain their composure when a grease fire starts in the kitchen, and they need to reassure diners to remain calm.

The pilot's experience in the Peace Corps may have honed his problem-solving skills and his ability to inspire others to be good workers. His years in his father's delicatessen would never appear on his professional pilot's résumé, but this expertise will be invaluable in assuring investors and lenders that he knows how to buy food in bulk and run a cash register.

The information you provide in the text of your business plan will help you expand on your résumé and convince others that you have acquired particularly useful skills that will make your business a success.

Here are some additional points to follow in describing your experience:

Style. Most business plans use the third person in discussing the qualifications of the entrepreneur seeking financial support. The pilot will probably refer to himself throughout his plan by his last name only, after introducing his full name near the beginning of the text. Employing the first person *I* in the body of the text is, however, a growing trend. The advantage is that it reinforces your role as the key person in your venture's success. However, if you have an equal partner in the business, stick to the third person, which indicates that neither owner will dominate, and that your relationship with each other will be balanced and well defined.

Placement. Presenting yourself in the best light is extremely important. Work to keep the description of your skills and experience in the executive summary as concise as possible. But make certain the text of your plan, and the information in your résumé, reflect the basic thrust of your sales pitch about yourself. Place each of these side by side, and read them one after the other to make certain the accomplishments you stress in the executive summary are reinforced in the text and in your résumé.

Honesty. Be honest about your skills, but don't oversell or undersell yourself. You are not boasting when you claim particular talents or expertise. Stressing your strengths reassures potential funders that you have the ability and experience to succeed, but if you go overboard, you will raise serious doubts about your honesty. Even if you began a business that failed, it is far better to mention it in your plan in a positive light than to hide the fact and have it emerge later.

Many successful entrepreneurs have failed in earlier attempts to start a business, but learned from their experiences. Milton Hershey, of chocolate bar fame, founded several candy companies that went belly up before he adopted a Swiss candy maker's process of combining milk with chocolate. Emphasize what you learned about running a business, hiring employees, attracting funding sources, being a boss or figuring out the right recipe. If your new venture builds on what you've learned, negative experiences will appear positive.

Amplification. The text is the place to expand on the basic information you outline in your résumé. Investors and lenders may not understand your background well enough to grasp the additional expertise you learned from a particular job. Remember the entrepreneur who wanted to buy a larger, more modern ocarina factory? Merely listing the fact that she played in an ocarina concert band on her résumé won't explain all the skills she acquired. Investors and lenders unfamiliar with the instrument may not understand how much she learned about dealing with artistic temperaments, or working as part of a team to achieve a cohesive musical presentation, or what qualities other ocarina performers admired and preferred in their instruments. This is the kind of résumé amplification you need to provide in the text of your business plan.

Your Résumé

Your résumé should be organized to emphasize your skills, experience, education, and training. Do not slip your standard professional résumé into the appendix of your business plan. Write a new one from scratch that stresses the credentials that make you absolutely the best person to start and grow your business.

Creating an effective résumé is an art. Like your overall business plan, your résumé must be neat, well designed, and free of spelling errors. It should have enough white space to make it easy to read and it should employ bullets, boldface, and underlining to emphasize important elements, such as the names of your previous employers and your job titles.

This is not the place for you to list or to proclaim unrelated professional or personal skills. You may have had the best baseball card collection in your neighborhood or bowled 300 twenty times in your league last year, but if these accomplishments have no bearing on your ability to start and expand a business, leave them out. However, if you have an interest that may not have appeared on a previous résumé, but adds to the case you're making about your qualifications, include it now.

The airline pilot with the plan for the pancake restaurant may have earned money towards his college tuition by waiting tables in the school cafeteria, in addition to working in his father's deli. His résumé might also include the leadership-training workshop he recently completed. These experiences have no place on his pilot's résumé, but they certainly indicate that he knows the food industry from the ground up, and that he's committed to polishing his managerial skills.

Here are some finer points of résumé creation:

Be simple. Keep it to one page. This is a quick overview to remind readers of your basic skills and experience. Even if you feel compelled to list every one of the 155 weddings at which your band performed to establish its popularity, don't do it here. Name a couple of the famous brides and grooms and list the total number; however, if potential investors want a more complete list, attach it to your appendix or mail it to them later. Don't try to be slick or snazzy by using special paper or fancy fonts. A résumé should impress people with its content, neatness and readability, not by multicolored headings or a typeface that looks like calligraphy.

Be clear. Choose the right format for your résumé that expresses your experience in the most powerful way possible. The organization of your skills and expertise must emphasize the qualities you wish to highlight for your readers. There are three basic formats to follow:

- **The chronological format** lists your work experience from the most recent job, placed first, back to your first job, which is placed last. It also includes the specific lengths of time you worked at each position.

This is the most common type of résumé, but it may not stress the skills you wish to emphasize to potential funders. It's a good exercise to create a résumé in this format, so you can scan your complete employment history on one page and choose which experiences you want to highlight in a more effective version.

- **The functional format** organizes your experience and employment under particular headings according to the type of positions you held. This format allows you to group related skills, even if they were acquired during part-time jobs or from purely personal interests. Dates are not usually included in this format. Compiling your background by function enables you to present your skills in a more interesting and compelling manner.

- **The targeted format** focuses even more closely on the specific skills needed for your particular venture. If all your past experience has been in the same field, each position has moved you higher on the professional ladder, and starting your own business is simply a culmination of your entire career, you probably won't need either the chronological or the functional format; the targeted design will work best for you.

Be consistent. Keep the style similar to the tone and language of your business plan text. Use parallel construction in verbs, so that you describe your duties in each of your jobs with similar tenses. If you use the past tense under one position, such as "coordinated travel schedules for a touring ocarina concert band," don't employ the present tense in another job description, unless you are still in that position, such as "analyze customer-service staff effectiveness." However, when you mention in your résumé that business you founded that failed, all you have to do is list the information without discussing the outcome.

Be animated. Use action verbs and an active voice to describe your duties at each of your jobs. Words such as *achieved, devised,* or *pioneered* express power and accomplishment. Phrases should be short and to the point. Avoid complete sentences or paragraphs. Omit professional abbreviations or jargon that potential funders might not recognize. Never use the first person to discuss your skills and accomplishments in your résumé.

Be careful. Check your grammar, spelling, indents, and layout. Then check them again, then one more time. Give your résumé to someone else, preferably an English teacher or a professional editor, to make sure you haven't committed some terrible error that will ruin your credibility in an instant—or in a punctuation mark.

Be honest. Your résumé should be scrupulously honest. It is standard practice for many funding sources to check statements made on résumés. Don't say "Vice President" if you were Assistant Vice President, or "supervised staff of 12," when it was actually 10. I know of several aspiring entrepreneurs who had their deals derailed by this kind of inaccuracy, including a lawyer who claimed he graduated from Princeton when he had not. His funders, who were ready to write a check, liked him, his idea, and his references. Nothing on his résumé would have changed their minds—except a lie.

Remember that you are selling potential investors and lenders on you and your abilities, not just on your business idea. You must impress people you want to support your venture that you—and your team— are uniquely qualified to establish this company and make it profitable. This is not gloating or boasting; this is the way to reassure funders that you have the background, talent, and enthusiasm to make your enterprise successful.

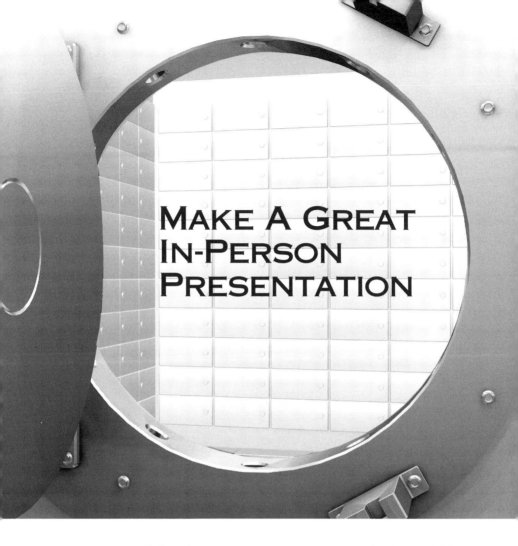

MAKE A GREAT IN-PERSON PRESENTATION

Despite all the electronic communication methods available today, nothing is more effective than an in-person meeting. In fact, it is unlikely that you will raise funds from investors or a bank without meeting them in person. An in-person meeting gives you the chance to reinforce key points of your plan, respond to questions, discover more about the potential funder's goals, and learn what did not come across well in the plan. It also gives you the opportunity to demonstrate the personal characteristics that lenders and investors want to see in an entrepreneur before writing a check.

As you prepare for an in-person presentation, keep in mind that you will need to understand and manage the Three Cs of any business meeting: *Context, Content* and *Code*.

Context

The most productive meetings occur when the atmosphere, or context, is conducive to having an open, honest discussion about mutually beneficial goals. Your attitude, your ability to listen and your understanding of the physical setting, will help you create an effective context for your presentations.

Attitude. Your own individual perspective, or point of view, that you bring to every meeting is an important factor in establishing a productive context. You need to be thoroughly prepared and know that you are thoroughly prepared. You must be confident that the plan you're presenting is strong and can benefit the people listening to your presentation. You must be open to answering questions—and to asking questions—so you can understand the funders' or investors' goals.

Listening. A critical element of creating a successful context revolves around thoughtful and attentive listening. By being a good listener, you allow the other people in the meeting to feel comfortable about sharing information openly. This enables you to uncover their professional concerns more readily and respond to them effectively. The presentation of a business plan is not a one-sided performance; it's a meeting to determine if you and the potential investors or funders want to work together to produce a mutually beneficial venture.

Setting. Since you'll probably be meeting in the bankers' or investors' offices, you will have minimal control over your physical surroundings. However, there are ways you can enhance the setting. First of all, arrive on time. No matter how pleasant the office may be, the meeting cannot proceed comfortably if you're late. If you're too early, don't hang around the waiting room looking like a person with nothing else to do. Go sit in your car or a nearby coffee shop. When you're ushered into the meeting, try to choose a seat which gives you the best angle for making eye contact with all the others in the room without pivoting your head too much. Take out your cell phone or PDA, turn it off, and place it on the table to indicate your willingness to concentrate solely on the matters at hand.

When you have the right attitude, listen fully, and create the most effective setting possible, you are establishing a strong context and demonstrating that you're worthy of other people's time and attention.

Content

The subject matter of your presentation should always be focused on the topics that are most crucial to the other people in the room. Whether you're meeting with bankers or potential investors, you must address their separate and measurable goals in your presentation. This includes such subjects as being able to pay back a bank loan within a certain time period, or projecting the return on an investor's stake—in other words, how your business will make money for them. Many entrepreneurs waste the opportunities intrinsic to an in-person presentation by concentrating solely on their own goals rather than focusing on the bankers' or investors' objectives.

Start strong and end strong. Research shows that people tend to form opinions based on what they hear at the beginning and the end of any meting. These tendencies, called the *primacy* and *recency* effects, are powerful tools. Be sure to put what you believe is your strongest point first in a presentation and to conclude with the same point, or with an equally strong message.

Customize your presentation. Don't waste bankers' time detailing the equity returns that your investors will earn, or bore your potential investors by describing your employees' stock options. These points may merit quick summaries in every presentation, but tailor the information for each group or individual. Make a list of the issues that are most important to your specific audience before your meeting and focus on those topics.

Don't create a Broadway production. People seem to think that the proverbial dog-and-pony show needs a high level of production values in order to appear professional and credible. This may be true for the weak presenter who has little to say if the slide projector goes dim, but for someone who has created a quality bankable business plan, there are several significant reasons to avoid dependence on these devices:

- The slide show or PowerPoint presentation can't be changed easily on the fly. It does not allow you to alter your presentation to incorporate new issues or a particular focus that might emerge through discussions with bankers or investors.

- Using visual presentation tools discourages people from talking, because they know that you're essentially following a script. You are, therefore, stifling one of the greatest assets of the in-person meeting: the opportunity to elicit productive discussion and address any questions that may arise.

- Many people don't pay attention to presentations that aren't interactive. Dim the lights, turn on the projector, and most people will tune out. An interactive presentation can only occur if your audience is involved, not passively watching a performance.

Keep the exposition of your plan simple and flexible. PowerPoint slides or projections can work only if you're prepared to adjust the order of your material, or skip some parts entirely as you're making your presentation. Maximize the value of your in-person time with bankers or investors by encouraging them to focus on their important issues.

Code

Nonverbal means of communication, such as body language and facial expressions that occur during any in-person meeting, comprise the code. During your presentation you will be sending and receiving innumerable code transactions. Misinterpreting this unspoken dialogue can lead to feelings of rejection that may interfere with your ability to make an effective presentation and can be disastrous.

Seeing is not always believing. Many presentations are de-railed because the presenters become unnerved by how their audiences behave and not by what they say. People coming and going, looking bored or angry, or taking a challenging tone when asking questions can make presenters feel that they have already failed before they've even begun to talk. However, interpreting body language alone is not always an accurate guide to determining the other person's interest or intentions. I once attended a 20-minute sales presentation to a buyer who never once looked up from a game of solitaire on his computer. The presenter plugged along, befuddled by the buyer's rude and strange behavior. Much to the presenter's astonishment, the buyer agreed to the purchase at the end of the presentation.

Don't be prejudiced. A similar problem occurs if you pre-judge your audience. You may make a presentation to a group of young, arrogant MBAs, who annoy you by the disdainful tone of their comments. The question you need to ask yourself is, "Would it be okay if these people liked my business plan and gave me the resources I need to create my company?" If the answer is "yes," as I assume it would be, that you would be happy for their participation, then you need to work on understanding and controlling your prejudices.

Your mother was right: first impressions count. When your mother said "You only get one chance to make a good first impression," she was absolutely right. Research shows that within the first minute of meeting someone, people form an enduring opinion.

In studying the interviewing process, University of Toledo psychologist, Professor Frank Bernieri, documented the extraordinarily rapid pace at which people form first impressions. Bernieri discovered that people who watched video clips of job applicants simply enter a room and shake hands with the interviewer reached virtually the same conclusions about that person as the trained and experienced interviewer did after a 15-minute interview.

The impact of this on presenting your plan is tremendous. That initial impression made in less than the first minute will largely determine what the other person thinks of you. You need to use that first 60 seconds to every advantage. You might be the most organized person in the world, but if you're late to an appointment because of unforeseen traffic and are forced to climb seven flights of stairs because the elevator is broken, you will walk into the other person's office sweaty and out of breath, creating a long lasting impression of being disorganized.

To improve that crucial first impression you make, be aware of it. Many people have no idea how they come across to others, and often impress people quite differently than they intended. People may feel they present themselves as aggressive or ambitious, but actually appear soft spoken and timid to others.

Ask some people who will be candid to the point of pain to participate in a exercise with you. Schedule meetings either at their offices or homes and ask them to describe your manner, your clothes, your posture, and your speech *one minute after your arrival.* An even more helpful demonstration is to videotape yourself in a similar business practice session so you can draw your own conclusions about the impression you make. And, if necessary, fix it!

Practice. If you are not too experienced in giving presentations, or you are worried about being nervous, or just want to be as well-prepared as possible, be sure to practice in front of friends, colleagues, the mirror, or that video camera you used for testing the first impression you made. This will help you master the flow and facts of your presentation, and you'll be able to focus on addressing the specific needs and interests of your audience. It is generally a good idea to keep an outline and a copy of your full plan in front of you so you don't skip any important points or can find your place if you get lost.

Just be yourself. Many entrepreneurs believe that in order to convince others to invest in their ventures they must be forceful and manipulative, even if those qualities are not part of their personalities. However, there is absolutely no reason to be anyone other than yourself while making an in-person presentation. You have probably written your plan with yourself in mind as the founder and president of your company, and the plan already has a section explaining your—and your team's—qualifications.

You don't need to be a Nobel Prize-winning scientist, an Olympic gold medalist, or the global entrepreneur of the year. You don't even have to be a bulldozing salesperson, you just have to project a credible level of experience, knowledge, and professionalism.

I have seen too many entrepreneurs try to be formal when they are usually relaxed, funny when they are essentially serious, or pushy when they are really quite unassuming. All they achieved was a level of discomfort in the role they were playing, which interfered with their ability to communicate their enthusiasm for their ventures.

You simply need to demonstrate that you are the right person to start this company.

Leave something behind—the right something! Handing a copy of your plan, financial projections or background materials to the people who just heard your presentation is effective and often expected, but it's better to leave nothing than to leave documents that do not reflect specific issues discussed in the meeting.

Let's suppose you're presenting your plan to a bank for a loan. You have prepared your financial projections under the assumption that the bank will lend 80 percent of your fixed asset valuation. In the meeting, however, you learn that they'll actually lend 90 percent. Having the wrong projections in your file may hurt your chances of receiving the best loan. It's better to revise your projections after the meeting and deliver the documents that accurately reflect your in-person presentation a few days later. Handing out a business card will do quite nicely until you can deliver your strongest materials.

Establish a schedule for follow up. Take out your calendar at the end of your presentation so you can arrange a date by which you will hear the investors' or funders' decision about supporting your venture. As the meeting winds down, state clearly when you will deliver any revised financial projections, and confirm which materials you need from the investors or lenders, such as their sample contracts or agreements, references of people in whom they have invested, and feedback on your financial projections. Then establish what will happen next.

In my experience, it's most important to get a commitment on a fixed response date. Having a specific deadline gives you a valid reason to make a timely followup call.

An effective in-person presentation should follow the same logical organization of your business plan by moving from the general to the specific. Remember the Three Cs of any meeting—Context, Content and Code—so you maintain as much control as possible over the impact of your presentation. Allow enough time for questions, but don't misinterpret the tone of voice or body language of your audience. Being enthusiastic and knowledgeable about your plan and your presentation will convey your determination to bring success to your company, as well as to your lenders and investors.

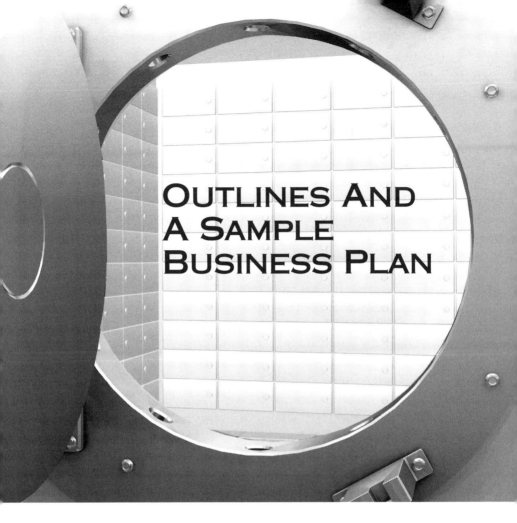

OUTLINES AND A SAMPLE BUSINESS PLAN

A plan can be short, sweet, and very effective. I have seen many compelling plans comprised of only four or five pages of text, followed by an appendix with a few financial projections. A simple plan is usually better if you can cover all the important issues in a few pages. It's easier to read, and will take less time to write. On the other hand, if you want to start a business which will have lengthy developmental phases, or various products sold in numerous markets, or a complicated manufacturing system protected by several patents, you will probably require a much longer, more complex plan.

As you read through the following outlines and sample plan, remember that these are examples, not templates. They are models to read and analyze, not formulas to copy. Your bankable business plan must be uniquely yours.

The best way to shape your plan is by creating a detailed outline. This will ensure that you have included all pertinent information in an organized fashion, with a strong executive summary near the beginning, have all necessary documents in the appendices, and prepared a clear, clean Cover Sheet. The following sample outlines were designed to summarize both a simple plan and a complex plan for two very different companies.

Outline For A Simple Business Plan

Remember that the exact headings of the subjects, and even whether these subjects should exist in your outline, depend on the specifics of your business and the purpose of your plan.

I. **Cover Sheet**
   A. Essential information, arranged from the top of the page to the bottom, in this order:
      1. Name of your company
      2. One sentence statement about your company
      3. Your name and any partners' names
      4. Contact name and information including telephone, fax, e-mail and mailing address
      5. Current month and year

II. **Table of Contents**
   A. List of key sections and appendices
   B. Add page numbers on which they appear

III. **Executive Summary (less than one page)**
   A. Statement of business opportunity
   B. Statement of what you require in loans or investments
   C. Purpose of plan
   D. Expected financial results
   E. Compare against the Ten Action Steps to make certain all are covered

IV. **Description of the Business**
   A. Product/service description and strengths
   B. For existing business, give history and financial performance
   C. Organization of the business, including management and ownership
   D. Legal structure

V. **Market Overview**
   A. Describe target market by geography, income, and demographics
   B. Competitive products, current buying patterns and market trends

VI. **Industry Overview**
   A. Competitors' history, products, and financial performance
   B. Trends, such as product changes, technology adoption, or consolidation
   C. Projections for the future
   D. Regulatory issues

VII. **Business Opportunity**
   A. Business strategy
   B. Product/service strengths
   C. Marketing and sales strategies
   D. Research to support projections
   E. Time line for starting and operating business

VIII. **Financial Projections**
   A. Statements
      1. Historical financial statements, if business exists
      2. Projected financial statements:
         a. Income statements

      b. Balance sheets
      c. Cash flow statements
      d. Debt-service projections
      e. Comparisons to industry standards
      f. Returns analysis

B. Six Key Financial Assumptions
   1. Startup costs
   2. Sales and revenue
   3. Operating costs
   4. Borrowing
   5. Equity returns
   6. Company value

IX. Appendices
   A. Résumés of key managers
   B. Newspaper, magazine articles; industry trade reports
   C. Key contracts, such as leases, employee agreements
   D. More detailed financials for the business
   E. Research to support projections

Outline For A Complex Business Plan

This outline is a comprehensive list of subjects you may wish to include in your plan. No plan needs to be this detailed, but you should read the outline and select those topics that relate to your business. Some topics are repeated because they should be considered in multiple areas, such as pricing and descriptions of competitors, but duplicating these issues in your final business plan is not necessary.

I. Cover Sheet
   A. Essential information, arranged from the top of the page to the bottom, in this order:
      1. Name of your company

    2. One sentence statement about your company
    3. Your name and any partners' names
    4. Contact name and information including telephone, fax, e-mail and mailing address
    5. Current month and year

II. Table of Contents
  A. List of key sections and appendices
  B. Add page numbers on which they appear

III. Executive Summary (less than one page)
  A. The Purpose of the Plan
    1. To obtain a bank loan
    2. To attract investors
    3. To document an operational plan for controlling the business
    4. To test the financial feasibility of a business concept
    5. To attract partners, vendors, or suppliers
  B. The Company
    1. Overview of the needs the company will meet
    2. The products or services you will offer
    3. Legal structure
  C. Market Analysis
    1. The characteristics of your target market (demographic, geographic, etc.)
    2. The size of your target market
  D. Market Research
    1. Market research that you have carried out to test and prove key elements of your plan including product or service characteristics, location viability, pricing, packaging, or target market acceptance
  E. Product or Service Research and Development
    1. Major milestones in product development and progress in meeting them

    F. Marketing and Sales Activities
1. Marketing strategy
2. Sales strategy
3. Keys to success in your competitive environment
4. Sales and marketing efforts to date

    G. Organization and Personnel
1. Key managers, owners, directors, advisors and employees
2. Organizational structure

    H. Financial Data
1. Funds required and their use
2. Historical financial summary
3. Prospective financial summary (including a justification for prospective sales levels)
4. Projected returns for equity investors
5. Debt coverage levels

IV. Company Description

    A. Nature of Your Business
1. Marketplace needs to be satisfied
2. Method(s) of need satisfaction
3. Key specific customers or market niches

    B. Your Distinctive Competencies and Competitive Advantages (primary factors that will lead to your success)
1. Elements of superior customer-need satisfaction
2. Cost advantages, such as production/service delivery efficiencies
3. Personnel
4. Distribution
5. Marketing program
6. Sales organization
7. Patents, copyrights, brand names that you own
8. Location strengths

      9. Experience, knowledge, or reputation of founders

  C. Operational Strategies

      1. Organizational structure

      2. Key financial incentives for your employees, partners, distributors, market reps and sales force

      3. Control and feedback structures to ensure that goals are being met

      4. Accountants, lawyers, consultants, directors and the expertise they provide

V. Market Analysis

  A. Industry Description and Outlook

      1. Description of industry and primary competitors

      2. List of competitors, including their financial information, strategies, histories, competitive strengths and weaknesses, products, and pricing

      3. Size of the industry, currently, historically, and in projections

      4. Industry characteristics: history and trends

         a. Technology changes

         b. Life cycle (is industry growing, maturing, consolidating, shrinking?)

            1. Historically

            2. Currently

            3. In the future

      5. Major customer groups

         a. Businesses

         b. Governments

         c. Consumers

  B. Target Markets

      1. Description and characteristics of target markets

    a. Critical needs to be filled
    b. Extent to which those needs are currently being met
    c. Demographic characteristics such as age, gender, race, ethnicity
    d. Geographic location
    e. Purchase decision makers and influencers
    f. Seasonal/cyclical trends

2. Primary target market size
    a. Number of prospective customers
    b. Annual purchases of products or services meeting the same or similar needs as your products or services
    c. Geographic area
    d. Demographic characteristics
    e. Anticipated market growth

3. Market penetration goals
    a. Market share
    b. Number of customers
    c. Geographic coverage
    d. Rationale for market penetration estimates, including research, testing, and competitors' experiences

4. Pricing/gross margin targets
    a. Price levels
    b. Gross-margin levels
    c. Discount structure (volume, promptness, payment terms, etc.)

5. Methods by which specific members of your target market can be identified
    a. Directories
    b. Trade association publications
    c. Government documents

6. Media plan
    a. Publications
    b. Radio/television/Internet ads & promotion

      c. Sources of influence/advice
      d. Specific media plan including budgets, sample ad copy, and plan to monitor ad results
    7. Purchasing cycle of potential customers
    8. Key trends and anticipated changes within your primary target markets
    9. Secondary target markets and key attributes
      a. Needs
      b. Demographics
      c. Significant future trends

C. Market Test Results
    1. Information/demonstrations given to prospective customers
    2. Reaction of prospective customers
    3. Importance of satisfaction of targeted needs
    4. Test group's willingness to purchase products/services at various price levels

D. Lead Times (amount of time between customer order placement and product/service delivery)
    1. Initial orders
    2. Reorders
    3. Volume purchases

E. Competition
    1. Identification (by product line or service and market segment)
      a. Existing
      b. Market share
      c. Potential (How long will your window of opportunity last before your initial success breeds new competition? Who are your new competitors likely to be?)
      d. Direct
      e. Indirect
    2. Strengths (competitive advantages)
      a. Ability to satisfy customer needs

        b. Market penetration
        c. Track record and reputation
        d. Staying power (financial resources)
        e. Key personnel
    3. Weaknesses (competitive disadvantages)
        a. Ability to satisfy customer needs
        b. Market penetration
        c. Track record and reputation
        d. Staying power (financial resources)
        e. Key personnel
    4. Importance of your target market to your competition
    5. Barriers to entry into the market
        a. Cost (investment)
        b. Time
        c. Technology
        d. Key personnel
        e. Customer inertia (brand loyalty, existing relationships, etc.)
        f. Existing patents and trademarks
F. Regulation
    1. Customer or governmental regulatory requirements
        a. Methods of meeting the requirements
        b. Timing involved in meeting the requirements
        c. Cost of meeting the requirements
    2. Anticipated changes in regulatory requirements
    3. Positives of regulations
        a. Barriers to entry for potential competitors
        b. Patent, copyright, trademark protection
        c. Government support of industry
        d. Trade protections for industry

VI. Products and Services

    A. Detailed Product/Service Description (from the users' perspective)
- 1. Specific benefits of product/service
- 2. Ability to meet needs
- 3. Competitive advantages
- 4. Present stage (idea, prototype, small production runs, etc.)

    B. Product Life Cycle
- 1. Describe the product/service's current position within its life cycle
- 2. Factors that might change the anticipated life cycle
  - a. Lengthen it
  - b. Shorten it

    C. Copyrights, Patents and Trade Secrets
- 1. Existing or pending copyrights or patents
- 2. Anticipated copyright and patent filings
- 3. Key aspects of your products or services which cannot be patented or copyrighted
- 4. Key aspects of your products or services which qualify as trade secrets
- 5. Existing legal agreements with owners and employees
  - a. Non-disclosure
  - b. Non-compete agreements

    D. Research and Development Activities
- 1. Activities in process at this time
- 2. Future activities (include milestones)
- 3. Anticipated results of future research and development activities
  - a. New products or services
  - b. New generations of existing products or services
  - c. Complimentary products or services
  - d. Replacement products or services

4. Research and development activities of others in your industry
   a. Direct competitors
   b. Indirect competitors
   c. Suppliers
   d. Customers

VII. **Marketing and Sales Activities**
   A. Overall Marketing Strategy
      1. Competitive advantages
         a. Pricing
         b. Delivery time
         c. Service
         d. Product features
         e. Brand name
         f. Reputation
         g. Status
      2. Market penetration strategy
         a. High profitability
         b. significant market share
      3. Growth strategy
         a. Internal
         b. Acquisition
         c. Franchise
         d. Horizontal (providing similar products to different users)
         e. Vertical (providing the products at different levels of the distribution chain)
      4. Distribution channels (include discount/profitability levels at each stage)
         a. Original equipment manufacturers
         b. Distributors
         c. Retailers
      5. Communication
         a. Promotion
         b. Advertising, including detailed media plan

       c. Public relations
       d. Personal selling
       e. Printed materials (catalogs, brochures, etc.)

B. Sales Strategies
  1. Sales force
    a. Internal vs. independent representatives (advantages and disadvantages of your strategy)
    b. Size
    c. Recruitment and training
    d. Compensation
  2. Prospecting
    a. Identifying prospects
    b. Prioritizing prospects
    c. Qualifying prospects (separating prospects from suspects)
  3. Sales activities
    a. Number of sales calls made per period
    b. Average number of sales calls per sale
    c. Average dollar size per sale
    d. Average dollar size per reorder

VIII. Operations

A. Production and Service Delivery Procedures
  1. Internal
  2. External (subcontractors)

B. Production/Service Delivery Capacity
  1. Internal
  2. External (subcontractors)
  3. Anticipated increases in capacity
    a. Investment
    b. New cost factors (direct and indirect)
    c. Logistics (will expansion force you to slow or stop production for a time?)
    d. Timing

C. Operating Competitive Advantages
    1. Techniques
    2. Experience
    3. Economies of scale
    4. Lower direct costs
D. Suppliers
    1. Identify suppliers of critical elements
        of production
        a. Primary
        b. Secondary
    2. Lead-time requirements
    3. Evaluate risks of critical element shortages
    4. Describe existing and anticipated contractual
        relationships with suppliers

IX. **Management and Ownership**
    A. Management Staff Structure
        1. Management staff organization chart
        2. Narrative description of the chart
    B. Key Managers (complete résumés should be
        presented in an appendix to the business plan)
        1. Name
        2. Position
        3. Primary responsibilities and authority
            in your company
        4. Primary responsibilities and authority
            with previous employers
        5. Unique skills and experiences that add to
            your company's distinctive competencies
        6. Compensation basis and levels
    C. Planned Additions to the Management Staff
        1. Position
        2. Primary responsibilities and authority
        3. Requisite skills and experience
        4. Recruitment process
        5. Timing of employment

6. Anticipated contribution to the company's success
7. Compensation basis and levels (be sure that they are in line with the market)

D. Legal Structure of the Business
1. Corporation
   a. C-corporation
   b. S-corporation
   c. Limited Liability Company (LLC)
2. Partnership
   a. General partnership
   b. Limited partnership
   c. Limited liability partnership
3. Sole Proprietorship

E. Owners
1. Names
2. Percentage of ownership
3. Extent of involvement with the company
4. Form of ownership
   a. Common stock
   b. Preferred stock
   c. General partner
   d. Limited partner
5. Outstanding equity equivalents
   a. options
   b. warrants
   c. convertible debt
6. Common stock
   a. authorized
   b. issued

F. Board of Directors
1. Names
2. Position on the board
3. Extent of involvement with the company
4. Backgrounds
5. Contribution to the company's success

a. Historically
b. In the future

X. **Organization and Personnel**
A. Complete Organization Chart
1. Positions
2. Reporting relationships
3. Narrative description of the organization chart
B. Brief Position Descriptions
1. Primary duties
2. Recruitment and training
3. Staffing levels
4. Compensation
a. Method
b. Level
C. Anticipated Human Resource Requirements
1. Organization chart
2. Staffing levels by position
3. Changes in compensation levels and/or methods

XI. **Funds Required and Their Uses**
A. Current Funding Requirements
1. Amount
2. Timing
3. Type
a. Equity
b. Debt
c. Mezzanine
4. Terms
B. Funding Requirements Over the Next Five Years
1. Amount
2. Timing
3. Type
a. Equity
b. Debt
4. Terms

C. Use of Funds
  1. Capital expenditures
  2. Working capital
  3. Debt retirement
  4. Acquisitions
D. Impact of the New Funds on the Company's Financial Position
  1. Dilution of ownership
  2. Change in leverage levels (debt to equity ratio)
E. Long-Range Financial and Exit Strategies
  1. Going public
  2. Leveraged buyout
  3. Acquisition by another company
  4. Debt service levels and timing
  5. Liquidation of the venture

XII. Financial Data
A. Historical Financial Data (past three to five years, if available)
  1. Annual summaries
     a. Income statement
     b. Balance sheet
     c. Cash flow statement or statement of changes in financial position
     d. Comparison to industry standards such as RMA data
  2. Level of CPA involvement (and name of firm)
     a. Audit
     b. Review
     c. Compilation
B. Prospective Financial Data (next five years)
  1. Next year (by month or quarter)
     a. Income statement
     b. Balance sheet
     c. Cash flow statement
     d. Capital expenditure budget

    e. Returns analysis
    f. Debt service schedule
   2. Remaining four years (by quarter and/or year)
    a. Income statement
    b. Balance sheet
    c. Cash flow statement
    d. Capital-expenditure budget
    e. Returns analysis
    f. Debt-service schedule
   3. Summary of significant assumptions
   4. Type of prospective financial data
    a. Forecast (management's best estimate)
    b. Projection (what-if scenarios)

XIII. Appendices or Exhibits
 A. Résumés of Key Managers
 B. Pictures of Products
 C. Professional References
 D. Market Studies
 E. Pertinent Published Information
   1. Magazine articles
   2. Books
 F. Patents
 G. Significant Contracts
   1. Leases
   2. Sales contracts
   3. Purchases contracts
   4. Partnership/ownership agreements
   5. Stock option agreements
   6. Employment/compensation agreements
   7. Non-compete agreements
   8. Insurance
    a. Product liability
    b. Officers' and directors' liability
    c. General liability
 H. Financial Commitments

1. Letters of intent from funding sources
2. Bank commitment letter
3. Letters of interest from potential customers

By the time you've completed your outline, the best length for your business plan should be apparent. Although most quality plans tend to be in the twenty to thirty page range, this is only a guideline, not a rule. Write your executive summary last, and make sure it covers all Ten Action Steps.

The following sample business plan for S & J Advertising is strong because it covers all Ten Action Steps in very few pages, but in a manner that a banker would be hard pressed to ignore. I adapted it from a similar plan created by a group of advertising executives lead by Neal Newman and Bill Parshall, two veteran broadcasters. They never executed this plan because other opportunities developed for them, but they passed it on to a group in another city that used it to build a successful agency.

S & J Advertising

A New Agency for the New Toledo

Sonica Smith and Sally Jones
Co-founders

Contact: Sonica Smith
Telephone: 419-123-4567 • Fax: 419-419-4199
E-mail: esseandjay@verizon.net

Mailing Address:
Sonica Smith
444 Advertising Road
Toldeo, OH 43605

Date: March 2007

S & J Advertising

Executive Summary

The purpose of this plan is to establish a strategy for the creation of S & J Advertising, a new agency that will be based in Toledo, Ohio. Sonica Smith and Sally Jones are the co-founders of S & J who, between them, bring nineteen years of experience in the Toledo advertising market to this venture. Their relationships with current advertisers will result in at least five clients coming to the firm at its inception. These five clients have given S & J letters stating this intent.

The co-founders' experience as professional and proven advertising executives will insure that their current clients will be satisfied, and that additional clients will join the S & J roster. Moreover, recent changes in the Toledo media market have created the need among advertisers for a firm of this caliber and expertise.

S & J expects to be profitable within its first year of operation, but seeks $50,000 in bank debt, for working capital and the construction of production facilities. The owners expect to personally guarantee this debt and to put in $50,000 of their own capital. The projections show that the company's cash flow will exceed debt service by a ratio of more than five to one in the first year and that the debt can be repaid within five years.

The Market

Toledo is an economically healthy and diverse market of more than 600,000 people located in northeastern Ohio. Major employers include Daimler Chrysler, Libbey Glass, Dana Corporation, and General Motors. There are more than 50,000 students enrolled in local institutions of higher learning, including Bowling Green College, the University of Toledo, and Owens Community College. For the last five years, unemployment has been consistently below 5 percent. Toledo has an opera company, a symphony orchestra, an art museum, a zoological society, a minor-league baseball team, and a regional airport.

The Advertising Market

The local advertising market has more than $150 million in annual revenue, and includes seven television stations, one local newspaper, and 20 radio stations. According to the 2006 Armstrong Radio Market Guide, the market revenues break down as follows:

Radio	$ 29	million
Television	56	million
Newspaper	54	million
Outdoor Advertising	7	million
Cable Television	4	million
Total	**$150**	**million**

Advertising Agency Competition

There are currently three advertising agencies in the Toledo area.

Bob Williams Advertising is a one-man shop that has been in business for 12 years and has three clients: a large local bakery, a car dealer, and a local bank.

Global Agency has been in business for five years, has six employees, and about 15 clients, including two car dealerships, a few restaurants, and a local college. They have video production capacity.

The Kryzyki Group has been in business for eight years, has three employees and ten clients, who mostly require copywriting services and print ad production. Clients are generally non-profits and educational establishments, including the opera, the symphony orchestra, the zoo, and a chain of day care centers.

The Current Opportunity

Various changes in the local media market have left local advertisers underserved.

Radio Consolidation

Over the last six years, the radio industry has gone through a major consolidation. As a result, two companies now have more than ninety percent of the radio revenue, each owning eight stations. To make this consolidation work, the radio companies have cut back on their production staffs and advertising reps. The remaining reps no longer have enough time to work with local advertisers on the creative and media planning aspects of their advertising expenditures. Production is more rushed, and sometimes is even issued from remote, centralized facilities which slows down the process and results in frequent mistakes, such as the mispronunciation of local proper names.

Media Service Reductions

In addition to this reduction in service from radio stations, local television, newspaper, and cable companies have all reduced the level of service to local advertisers, apparently as they push for higher profitability or respond to weak national trends in advertising.

The Rise of the Internet

Many businesses have websites and e-commerce strategies. Generally, local businesses rely upon computer-oriented people to build these web pages and do a poor job of integrating their Internet strategy with their overall advertising.

The opportunity that Smith and Jones have identified is the existence of many local advertisers who need and want higher levels of service, including the development and implementation of Internet strategies.

The Management Team

Sonica Smith holds a degree in advertising from Ohio State University and worked as an account representative for a local radio station for five years before becoming Sales Manager, a position she has held for the past four years.

Sally Jones was a local radio personality in Findlay, Ohio for seven years, which included responsibility for producing advertisements. She moved to Toledo ten years ago, and became the advertising manager for a local bank. In that capacity, she dealt with all the local media, developed the bank's website and completed courses in computer science and programming at the University of Toledo.

Smith and Jones are prepared to invest $25,000 each in the agency and to work at minimal salaries to keep the agency's break-even point low until the agency produces adequate profits to compensate them additionally.

Sales and Marketing Strategies

The sales and marketing strategies have already been established by commitments from five sizeable advertisers to engage S & J as their agency. These clients include the bank at which Sally Jones currently works, a local nightclub, two car dealerships, and a large outlet store. In the previous twelve months, these five businesses spent $1.1 million on advertising, not including website expenditures.

Smith and Jones have a target list of 23 additional advertisers that they know personally and believe will sign on as clients. They are currently meeting with each of these potential customers to tell them their plans, and try to obtain a commitment to join their roster of clients. Smith and Jones have identified an additional 135 potential clients in Toledo with annual advertising expenditures of $75,000 or more.

Company Structure

S & J will be a Limited Liability Company (LLC), so income will pass through to the two owners without being taxed at the company level, and to afford personal liability protection to both owners. Smith and Jones are currently working with a lawyer to draft the papers for the organization of the company, including an agreement between each of them to cover all contingencies in case one wishes to leave, or in the unlikely event that their working relationship deteriorates.

Capital Requirements

The appendix details the projected expenditures, including estimates from vendors, but Smith and Jones foresee the following basic capital requirements:

Computer hardware	$ 7,500
Computer software	1,500
Audio production studio	12,500
Video editing equipment	8,000
Office furniture	5,000
Total Financing Requirements	**$34,500**

Smith and Jones are seeking $50,000 in bank debt as working capital and to help build offices and production studios. They are willing to personally guarantee this loan. The attached tables show that the company will be profitable in the first year, and capable of handling this amount of debt.

Financial Projections

The attached projected financial statements make conservative assumptions for both revenue and expenses. They show S & J having an income of $23,485 in year one, and $32,325 and $65,040 in years two and three. The revenue projections assume that the company adds a net of eight new clients in year two and ten in year three. Given that five clients have already signed on, and that the company has a prime target list of 23 clients and an additional target list of 135 clients, this is also conservative. If, for any reason, the company does not meet its cash flow and profit targets, the principals are prepared to reduce their salaries.

The operating cash flow projections show that the company ends it first year of operation with a cash balance of $72,951, which is nearly six months of operating expense. The projections also show that the company will comfortably service debt, including repaying $10,000 in loan principal, at the end of year one. The ratio analysis and comparison with RMA data shows that the company is within the range for the average advertising agency, with the exception of having more cash than the average. It also has fewer short term liabilities than the average agency. This is likely due to the fact that the typical agency does much more expensive production than S & J expects to handle. S & J plans to focus more on time buying, which will result in a positive cash flow because time will not be ordered until S & J has received payment from the client. This focus also results in lower fixed-asset percentages than the average agency. The quick test ratio comprised of cash and net receivables divided by current liabilities similarly shows S & J to be more financially secure than the average agency.

The projections show that the S & J Advertising will be able to repay the loan in its fifth year.

S & J Advertising: Projected Profit and Loss

	Year 1	Year 2	Year 3
Revenue	150,000	270,000	405,000
Operating Expenses			
Salaries & Related expenses:			
Founders' payroll	60,000	80,000	120,000
Employees' payroll	0	55,000	82,500
Benefits and employee taxes	21,000	47,250	70,875
Total Salary and Related Expenses	81,000	182,250	273,375
Office Expenses:			
Rent	12,000	14,400	16,800
Communication	7,200	8,400	9,600
Advertising and website	5,400	7,200	12,000
Subscriptions	840	1,200	1,560
Misc. office expenses	1,200	2,400	2,400
Insurance and legal fees	4,800	4,800	4,800
Depreciation	3,075	5,225	7,425
Utilities	1,200	1,800	1,800
Other	4,800	6,000	7,200
Total Office Expenses	40,515	51,425	63,585
Total Operating Expenses	121,515	233,675	336,960
Income From Operations	28,485	36,325	68,040
Interest Expenses	(5,000)	(4,000)	(3,000)
Net Income	23,485	32,325	65,040

Assumptions

1. The company earns 15% commission on placed advertising.
2. First year company commissions are $150,000 from five already committed clients.
3. The company projects that its advertising contracts volume will increase:
   – in 2nd year by 80% by adding 8 new clients.
   – in 3rd year by 60% by adding 10 new clients.
4. Company pays bills in 35 days and receives payment in 45 days.
5. Income and expenses are spread evenly through the year.
6. Owners purchase $50,000 in common stock and guarantee $50,000 loan.
7. Because S & J is an LLC, income taxes are paid personally by owners.

S & J Advertising: Operating Expenses Detail

Salaries & Related Expenses:

	Year 1	Year 2	Year 3
Smith	30,000	40,000	60,000
Jones	30,000	40,000	60,000
Secretarial	0	20,000	30,000
Salesperson	0	35,000	52,500
Salary Total	60,000	135,000	202,500
Benefits and payroll taxes @35%	21,000	47,250	70,875
Total Personnel Expenses	**81,000**	**182,250**	**273,375**

Monthly Office & General Expenses

	Year 1	Year 2	Year 3
Rent	1,000	1,200	1,400
Communication: wireless & mail	600	700	800
Advertising and website	450	600	1,000
Subscriptions	70	100	130
Office expenses	100	200	200
Insurance & legal Fees	400	400	400
Utilities	100	150	150
Other	400	500	600
Total Monthly Office Expenses	**3,120**	**3,850**	**4,680**
Total Yearly Office Expenses	**37,440**	**46,200**	**56,160**

Interest Expenses

	Year 1	Year 2	Year 3
Bank loan outstanding	50,000	40,000	30,000
Principal repaid	10,000	10,000	10,000
Principal remaining at year end	40,000	30,000	20,000
Interest @10%	5,000	4,000	3,000

S & J Advertising: Projected Balance Sheet as of Year End

Assets	Year 1	Year 2	Year 3
Current Assets:			
Cash & cash equivalents	72,951	107,185	180,790
Accounts receivable	26,719	35,438	37,969
Other short-term assets	8,000	8,000	8,000
Total current assets	107,670	150,623	226,759
Fixed assets:			
Furniture & equipment cost	34,500	46,000	57,000
Less accumulated depreciation	3,075	8,300	15,725
Total fixed assets	31,425	37,700	41,275
Other Assets:			
Other assets and misc. investments	1,000	1,000	1,000
Total Other Assets	1,000	1,000	1,000
Total Assets	140,095	189,323	269,034

Liabilities & Stockholders' Equity

	Year 1	Year 2	Year 3
Current liabilities:			
Accounts payable	26,610	53,513	78,184
Short-term bank borrowing	0	0	0
Other short-term liabilities	0	0	0
Total Current Liabilities	26,610	53,513	78,184
Noncurrent liabilities:			
Long-term debt	40,000	30,000	20,000
Total Non-current Liabilities	40,000	30,000	20,000
Stockholders' equity:			
Common stock	50,000	50,000	50,000
Retained earning	0	23,485	55,810
Income	23,485	32,325	65,040
Total Stockholders' Equity	73,485	105,810	170,850
Total Liabilities & Stockholders' Equity	140,095	189,323	269,034

S & J Advertising: Cash Flow Statement

	Year 1	Year 2	Year 3
Net Profit	**23,485**	**32,325**	**65,040**
Plus:			
Depreciation	3,075	5,225	7,425
Change in accounts payable	26,610	26,903	24,671
Increase (decrease) other liabilities	0	0	0
Increase (decrease) long-term borrowing	40,000	(10,000)	(10,000)
Capital investment	50,000	0	0
Subtotal	**119,685**	**22,128**	**22,096**
Less:			
Change in accounts receivable	26,719	8,719	2,531
Change in other assets	8,000	0	0
Fixed assets	34,500	11,500	11,000
Change in other assets	1,000	0	0
Subtotal	**70,219**	**20,219**	**13,531**
Net Cash Flow	**72,951**	**34,234**	**73,605**
Cash Balance	**72,951**	**107,185**	**180,790**

S & J Advertising: Fixed Asset Detail

	Year 1	Year 2	Year 3
Furniture & Equipment Open Balance			
Computer hardware	7,500	0	0
Computer software	1,500	0	0
Audio production software	12,500	0	0
Video editing equipment	8,000	0	0
Office furniture	5,000	0	0
Leasehold improvement	0	0	0
Total	**34,500**	**0**	**0**
Purchasing			
Computer hardware	0	10,000	10,000
Computer software	0	500	1,000
Audio production software	0	0	0
Video editing equipment	0	0	0
Office furniture	0	0	0
Leasehold improvement	0	1,000	0
Total Purchasing	**0**	**11,500**	**11,000**
Furniture & Equipment Closing Balance			
Computer hardware	7,500	17,500	27,500
Computer software	1,500	2,000	3,000
Audio production software	12,500	12,500	12,500
Video editing equipment	8,000	8,000	8,000
Office furniture	5,000	5,000	5,000
Leasehold improvement	0	1,000	1,000
Total Fixed Assets	**34,500**	**46,000**	**57,000**

Depreciation	*% Per Year*			
Open balance		0	3,075	8,300
Yearly				
Computer hardware	20%	1,500	3,500	5,500
Computer software	20%	300	400	600
Audio production software	5%	625	625	625

S & J Advertising: Fixed Asset Detail (cont.)

		Year 1	Year 2	Year 3
Video editing equipment	5%	400	400	400
Office furniture	5%	250	250	250
Leasehold improvement	5%	0	50	50
Total Yearly Depreciation		**3,075**	**5,225**	**7,425**
Total Accumulated Depreciation		**3,075**	**8,300**	**15,725**

The following four pages from the current RMA Annual Statement Studies indicate that the financial projections for S & J Advertising compare favorably to their average advertising agency data.

PROFESSIONAL SERVICES—Advertising Agencies   NAICS 541810 (SIC 7311)

	Current Data Sorted By Assets							Comparative Historical Data	
Type of Statement	0-500M	500M-2MM	2-10MM	10-50MM	50-100MM	100-250MM		4/1/00-3/31/01 ALL	4/1/01-3/31/02 ALL
		69 (4/1-9/30/04)		308 (10/1/04-3/31/05)					
Unqualified	1	2	15	12	1	1		23	17
Reviewed	3	19	39	10				82	65
Compiled	21	32	20	1		1		95	91
Tax Returns	47	25	2					52	36
Other	23	41	48	9	3	1		131	142
NUMBER OF STATEMENTS	95	119	124	32	4	3		383	351
	%	%	%	%	%	%		%	%
ASSETS									
Cash & Equivalents	20.4	14.9	19.2	18.0				12.8	15.3
Trade Receivables (net)	28.8	47.0	55.5	47.5				47.6	45.9
Inventory	2.5	4.2	3.1	6.2				3.1	2.1
All Other Current	4.2	4.5	3.3	3.3				4.1	4.0
Total Current	56.0	70.6	81.1	75.0				67.6	67.2
Fixed Assets (net)	28.3	16.1	10.6	7.2				18.7	18.8
Intangibles (net)	4.5	4.3	2.6	11.6				5.4	6.3
All Other Non-Current	11.3	9.0	5.8	6.2				8.3	7.7
Total	100.0	100.0	100.0	100.0				100.0	100.0
LIABILITIES									
Notes Payable-Short Term	25.6	13.9	6.5	3.6				14.2	10.1
Cur. Mat.-LT/D	5.9	3.9	2.0	1.2				2.5	3.2
Trade Payables	22.2	30.8	34.9	38.5				31.2	32.9
Income Taxes Payable	.2	.3	.6	.8				.5	.4
All Other Current	18.1	15.7	18.5	29.4				17.4	18.8
Total Current	72.0	64.6	62.5	73.5				65.7	65.3
Long-Term Debt	29.4	13.4	5.7	3.2				10.6	11.0
Deferred Taxes	.1	.4	.2	.2				.6	.3
All Other Non-Current	10.1	6.5	5.4	3.3				4.4	4.3
Net Worth	-11.7	15.2	26.2	19.8				18.7	19.2
Total Liabilities & Net Worth	100.0	100.0	100.0	100.0				100.0	100.0
INCOME DATA									
Net Sales	100.0	100.0	100.0	100.0				100.0	100.0
Gross Profit									
Operating Expenses	95.1	96.2	93.9	95.6				95.6	97.7
Operating Profit	4.9	3.8	6.1	4.4				4.4	2.3
All Other Expenses (net)	1.8	.7	.4	.6				1.2	1.2
Profit Before Taxes	3.0	3.1	5.7	3.8				3.2	1.1
RATIOS									
Current	1.9	1.7	1.8	1.1				1.6	1.5
	1.1	1.1	1.2	1.0				1.1	1.1
	.4	.8	1.1	.9				.9	.8
Quick	1.7	1.6	1.6	1.1				1.5	1.3
	.9	1.0	1.2	.9				1.0	1.0
	.4	.7	.9	.6				.8	.7
Sales/Receivables	0 UND	34 10.9	40 9.0	45 8.1				32 11.4	28 12.8
	20 18.2	46 8.0	64 5.7	72 5.1				51 7.2	49 7.4
	39 9.4	69 5.3	87 4.2	107 3.4				78 4.7	74 4.9

PROFESSIONAL SERVICES—Advertising Agencies NAICS 541810 (SIC 7311)

Ratio								
Cost of Sales/Inventory	14.8 / 276.8 / -11.3		8.0 / 19.2 / 123.5		20.8 / NM / -20.1		12.5 / 57.2 / -41.4	
Cost of Sales/Payables	12.9 / 50.8 / -26.3		54.0 / 12.3 / 4.2		219.8 / 12.7 / 2.8			
Sales/Working Capital	8.2 / 3.4 / -1.3		19.1 / 5.3 / 1.1		20.5 / 4.3 / 1.9			
EBIT/Interest	(102) 4.1 / 1.5 / -.9	(12)	(95)	(23)			(316) 13.3 / 4.2 / 1.2	(281) 8.5 / 2.1 / -2.2
Net Profit + Depr., Dep., Amort./Cur. Mat. L./T/D	(12) 20.5 / 4.3 / 1.9						(73) 11.0 / 3.2 / 1.7	(57) 6.8 / 2.2 / .3
Fixed/Worth	.2 / 1.0 / -.7	.2 / .8 / -5.2	.1 / .4 / 1.2		.2 / .6 / 3.5		.3 / .8 / 7.0	.3 / 1.1 / -3.9
Debt/Worth	.9 / 3.6 / -2.8	1.5 / 4.5 / -31.4	1.5 / 3.5 / 13.0		4.9 / 8.7 / 125.4		1.3 / 4.0 / 83.5	1.7 / 5.0 / -18.3
% Profit Before Taxes/Tangible Net Worth	(87) 96.9 / 31.5 / 4.3	88.9 / 39.8 / 9.0	(108) 83.9 / 39.6 / 12.5	(25)	92.8 / 70.4 / 35.7		(291) 77.3 / 32.2 / 8.3	(243) 65.4 / 19.0 / -1.6
% Profit Before Taxes/Total Assets	33.3 / 8.1 / -5.9	20.2 / 6.9 / .3	22.6 / 10.2 / 2.2		14.0 / 6.9 / .3		17.9 / 6.0 / .7	12.3 / 2.3 / -3.8
Sales/Net Fixed Assets	141.3 / 31.6 / 12.4	103.1 / 30.1 / 13.9	106.9 / 52.7 / 24.1		99.5 / 36.9 / 13.8		66.3 / 29.3 / 13.2	68.0 / 29.5 / 12.8
Sales/Total Assets	9.1 / 4.4 / 3.1	4.8 / 3.4 / 2.2	4.5 / 3.3 / 2.2		3.3 / 2.3 / 1.1		5.3 / 3.5 / 2.3	5.2 / 3.5 / 2.2
% Depr., Dep., Amort./Sales	(54) 1.6 / 3.2 / .6	(95) .9 / 2.6	(101) .4 / 1.7	(23) .6 / 1.1 / 2.3			(308) .6 / 1.2 / 2.2	(281) .6 / 1.3 / 2.7
% Officers', Directors', Owners' Comp/Sales	(51) 11.2 / 19.6 / 5.7	(53) 6.2 / 9.8 / 3.4	(37) 2.3 / 3.3 / 7.0				(172) 3.6 / 6.3 / 11.6	(149) 3.9 / 7.5 / 13.6
Net Sales ($)	141965M	489780M	2016308M	1735006M	603610M	1400400M	6296183M	6422059M
Total Assets ($)	23463M	138783M	580143M	659471M	236038M	504572M	2730871M	2571225M

M = $ thousand MM = $ million

PROFESSIONAL SERVICES—Advertising Agencies   NAICS 541810   (SIC 7311)

	Comparative Historical Data			Current Data Sorted By Sales					
Type of Statement									
Unqualified	17	24	32		2		8	11	11
Reviewed	76	79	72	1	7	12	9	28	15
Compiled	62	98	74	13	17	13	15	10	6
Tax Returns	54	57	74	31	21	12	7	2	1
Other	104	123	125	11	31	16	24	27	16
	4/1/02-3/31/03 ALL	4/1/03-3/31/04 ALL	4/1/04-3/31/05 ALL	0-1MM	69 (4/1-9/30/04) 1-3MM	3-5MM	5-10MM	308 (10/1/04-3/31/05) 10-25MM	25MM & OVER
NUMBER OF STATEMENTS	313	381	377	56	78	53	63	78	49
ASSETS	%	%	%	%	%	%	%	%	%
Cash & Equivalents	16.7	16.0	18.1	22.2	13.9	18.1	16.0	19.3	21.3
Trade Receivables (net)	45.5	46.8	45.1	21.0	43.7	45.4	50.4	55.8	50.6
Inventory	2.9	2.9	3.5	2.3	4.1	3.8	3.2	4.0	3.4
All Other Current	4.4	4.8	4.0	6.4	3.5	5.2	3.2	2.4	4.2
Total Current	69.6	70.4	70.8	51.9	65.2	72.5	72.8	81.6	79.6
Fixed Assets (net)	18.1	14.7	16.6	34.1	19.5	14.1	15.6	8.6	8.8
Intangibles (net)	3.9	4.4	4.4	6.0	4.7	4.4	2.2	4.3	4.9
All Other Non-Current	8.4	10.4	8.3	8.1	10.7	9.0	9.5	5.5	6.7
Total	100.0	100.0	100.0	100.0	100.0	100.0	100.0	100.0	100.0
LIABILITIES									
Notes Payable-Short Term	14.2	12.6	13.4	23.5	16.5	17.1	11.1	8.5	4.1
Cur. Mat.-L/T/D	3.1	4.5	3.5	10.3	3.3	3.0	1.8	1.9	1.2
Trade Payables	32.7	32.5	30.8	19.0	23.9	36.5	31.3	35.7	40.6
Income Taxes Payable	.4	.5	.4	.3	.3	.1	.6	.5	.7
All Other Current	19.2	22.2	18.5	11.6	17.0	17.8	23.9	17.2	24.4
Total Current	69.7	72.3	66.6	64.7	60.9	74.5	68.9	63.8	71.0
Long-Term Debt	8.5	11.2	13.9	39.3	17.4	13.4	8.1	4.0	3.3
Deferred Taxes	.3	.6	.3	.2	.2	.2	.4	.3	.2
All Other Non-Current	4.7	3.8	6.7	11.7	5.7	9.6	3.1	6.0	5.1
Net Worth	16.7	12.1	12.5	-15.9	15.7	2.4	19.6	26.0	20.5
Total Liabilities & Net Worth	100.0	100.0	100.0	100.0	100.0	100.0	100.0	100.0	100.0
INCOME DATA									
Net Sales	100.0	100.0	100.0	100.0	100.0	100.0	100.0	100.0	100.0
Gross Profit									
Operating Expenses	96.2	96.2	95.1	90.7	96.9	96.6	95.3	94.7	96.2
Operating Profit	3.8	3.8	4.9	9.3	3.1	3.4	4.7	5.3	3.8
All Other Expenses (net)	1.0	1.0	.9	3.1	.7	.4	.2	.8	.1
Profit Before Taxes	2.9	2.9	4.0	6.2	2.5	3.0	4.5	4.5	3.7
RATIOS									
Current	1.6	1.6	1.7	2.4	2.0	1.7	1.5	1.6	1.3
	1.1	1.1	1.2	1.3	1.2	1.2	1.1	1.2	1.1
	.8	.8	.9	.4	.7	.8	.8	1.0	1.0
Quick	1.4	1.4	1.6	2.4	1.7	1.6	1.3	1.6	1.2
	1.0	1.0	1.1	.9	1.0	1.0	1.0	1.2	1.1
	.7	.7	.7	.4	.6	.7	.8	.9	.8

Each cell shows upper quartile / median / lower quartile (stacked top-to-bottom in the source). Values in parentheses are counts or days.

Ratio	Comparative 1	Comparative 2	Comparative 3	Current 1	Current 2	Current 3	Current 4	Current 5	Current 6
Sales/Receivables	(28) 13.0 / (47) 7.8 / (71) 5.2	(29) 12.6 / (52) 7.0 / (76) 4.8	(29) 12.8 / (46) 8.0 / (72) 5.1	(0) UND / (11) 33.4 / (38) 9.6	(30) 12.1 / (45) 8.1 / (69) 5.3	(32) 11.3 / (47) 7.8 / (78) 4.7	(34) 10.6 / (53) 6.8 / (94) 3.9	(39) 9.3 / (57) 6.4 / (82) 4.4	(32) 11.3 / (46) 7.9 / (67) 5.4
Cost of Sales/Inventory									
Cost of Sales/Payables									
Sales/Working Capital	14.1 / 88.8 / -32.1	13.0 / 93.0 / -24.8	11.9 / 46.0 / -31.5	11.2 / 73.8 / -7.2	10.9 / 93.0 / -17.4	8.9 / 46.6 / -35.2	13.5 / 33.3 / -26.3	11.0 / 27.8 / 231.7	15.8 / 61.4 / -106.8
EBIT/Interest	(257) 16.8 / 4.3 / .3	(304) 19.3 / 4.8 / -.7	(296) 23.8 / 7.1 / 1.6	(35) 9.0 / 2.9 / .7	(68) 15.8 / 4.1 / .9	(45) 18.1 / 4.4 / 1.3	(54) 29.8 / 11.6 / 1.1	(61) 74.6 / 11.0 / 2.8	(33) 67.6 / 15.6 / 7.8
Net Profit + Depr., Dep., Amort./Cur. Mat. L/T/D	(50) 7.7 / 2.0 / .4	(52) 8.5 / 3.7 / .7	(45) 19.6 / 4.3 / 1.4				(13) 21.6 / 4.3 / 1.4		(10) 27.7 / 19.3 / 4.5
Fixed/Worth	.3 / .8 / -11.8	.2 / .6 / 46.8	.2 / .5 / 5.7	.1 / 2.2 / -.4	.2 / .8 / -5.0	.2 / 1.1 / -1.5	.2 / .5 / 3.5	.1 / .3 / 1.8	.2 / .4 / 1.2
Debt/Worth	1.6 / 4.6 / -57.4	1.7 / 4.9 / -42.9	1.4 / 4.7 / 271.3	1.0 / 3.5 / -2.1	1.0 / 3.4 / -28.8	1.5 / 5.3 / -13.4	1.0 / 3.4 / 76.7	1.7 / 5.9 / 19.8	2.5 / 5.4 / 15.0
% Profit Before Taxes/Tangible Net Worth	(228) 77.6 / 27.7 / 3.6	(282) 87.5 / 27.5 / 2.5	(286) 89.3 / 40.8 / 9.2	(33) 113.5 / 47.6 / 9.0	(58) 78.5 / 28.5 / 2.2	(37) 72.8 / 33.3 / 8.3	(49) 106.2 / 45.4 / 13.2	(67) 128.8 / 40.7 / 12.2	(42) 92.7 / 52.2 / 21.9
% Profit Before Taxes/Total Assets	17.0 / 5.2 / -.5	16.4 / 4.5 / -1.1	21.0 / 8.1 / .5	42.1 / 10.2 / -1.7	20.9 / 6.9 / .0	14.2 / 5.1 / .6	27.7 / 8.4 / 1.2	25.4 / 9.1 / 1.9	15.4 / 7.9 / 1.6
Sales/Net Fixed Assets	74.7 / 34.0 / 13.7	97.9 / 39.5 / 17.6	106.2 / 40.0 / 15.3	127.3 / 20.2 / 4.6	78.3 / 25.5 / 11.4	108.7 / 30.1 / 13.7	103.1 / 30.7 / 18.6	117.0 / 53.6 / 25.5	124.9 / 62.0 / 34.1
Sales/Total Assets	5.1 / 3.7 / 2.4	5.1 / 3.5 / 2.2	4.9 / 3.5 / 2.2	6.2 / 3.2 / 1.2	4.6 / 3.5 / 2.1	4.6 / 3.3 / 2.1	4.9 / 3.3 / 2.4	5.0 / 3.8 / 2.4	5.8 / 4.1 / 2.6
% Depr., Dep., Amort./Sales	(260) .6 / 1.2 / 2.4	(299) .5 / 1.1 / 2.3	(278) .4 / 1.1 / 2.1	(29) 1.3 / 2.7 / 9.8	(53) .6 / 1.4 / 3.0	(44) .4 / .8 / 1.8	(53) .4 / 1.1 / 2.1	(65) .4 / .7 / 1.5	(34) .3 / .6 / 1.1
% Officers', Directors', Owners' Comp/Sales	(141) 3.1 / 6.1 / 11.0	(150) 2.8 / 7.4 / 12.9	(143) 3.2 / 6.4 / 11.8	(29) 8.2 / 14.4 / 20.8	(38) 4.5 / 8.7 / 11.9	(27) 3.4 / 4.7 / 7.5	(17) 2.9 / 6.7 / 9.7	(25) 2.2 / 3.1 / 4.6	
Net Sales ($)	7297368M	10158644M	6387069M	29452M	146834M	204451M	446987M	1228132M	4331213M
Total Assets ($)	1914921M	3183787M	2142470M	14744M	58669M	79039M	171645M	469289M	1349084M

M = $ thousand   MM = $ million

RESOURCES

I have a created a website with information and tools to supplement this book. It includes sample plans, links to other useful sites, a web-based automated business plan writing system and other material: ***www.bankablebusinessplans.com***.

Part II: Action Step 4: Analyze Your Market – Who Will Want Your Product Or Service?

The Encyclopedia of Associations, published by Thomson, is available in book form or on the web through libraries that subscribe to it. It is a good place to find your industry association that might publish industry background information.

The *Thomas Register of American Manufacturers* is similarly available in book form or free on the web at *www.thomasnet.com*. If you need to locate possible suppliers for your business, it is an efficient place to begin.

Start Your Own Business, 4th Edition, by Rieva Lesonsky, Entrepreneur Press, 2007. This book is a comprehensive guide to the process of starting your business.

Entrepreneur magazine's site, *www.entrepreneur.com*, is also extremely useful.

Hoover's at *www.hoovers.com*, provides company and industry data and various useful links. Some information is provided at no charge; other data is on a fee basis.

Financial and Operating Results of Department and Specialty Stores, published by the National Retail Merchants Association, is an annual presentation of detailed financial information that can serve as useful guidance and comparison.

The U.S. Census Bureau, at www.census.gov is a source for literally billions of dollars of high-quality research on population, industries, employment, and ethnic groups, most of which is available for all localities throughout the United States. Industry reports compiled by the Census Bureau can be searched by NAICS code (see Action Step 10 for an explanation of the coding systems at *www.census.gov/cir/www*). There is so much information, that it may take a while to sort through it all, but it's worth the time, and the price is right...it's free.

Other ways to search the vast array of government offerings include the Catalog of Federal Domestic Assistance at *www.cfda. gov*; the Government Printing Office at *www.gpo.gov*; FedStats at *www.fedstats.gov*; the National Associations of Counties at *www. naco.org*.

The Small Business Administration (*www.sba.gov*) is loaded with useful information, reports, financing worksheets, background on government programs, and many links. It is somewhat cumbersome to navigate, but worth the time. Some of the same information is available more directly through another SBA site, the U.S. Small Business Advisor (*www.sba.gov/smallbusiness-planner/plan/index.html*).

Information on public companies in your industry can provide good background or comparisons with your own plans. The Securities and Exchange Commission site, *www.sec.gov/info/edgar.shtml*, provides fast access to all public company filings.

Quicken and CNN, along with their websites, *www.quicken.com* and *www.money.cnn.com*, provide current and historical financial information for public companies.

Standard and Poor's has various industry reports at its site, *www.standardandpoors.com*.

General business background information is available through *www.factiva.com*, which is the site for searching the Reuters and Dow Jones business publications.

LexisNexis (*www.lexis.com*) offers data from public records, newspapers, and magazines.

Kompass at *www.kompass.com* provides product and contact information for 2 million companies throughout the world. Their Product/Services and Companies search engine is a valuable resource.

Moody's | Economy.com (*www.economy.com/freelunch*) offers links to nearly a million sources of economic and financial data on industries, consumers, and government statistics.

Many libraries offer information directly over the web, or provide links to business references. Among the better ones are:

The Library of Congress (*www.lcweb.loc.gov*)

U.S. Public Libraries on the Web (*www.lists.webjunction.org/ libweb/Public_main.html*)

The American Library Association guide to best business websites (*www.ala.org/rusa/brass/besthome.html*)

The Librarian's Index to the Internet (*www.lii.org*)

Some websites such as Factiva, Standard and Poor's, and Lex-isNexis charge for their use, but many libraries subscribe to such services and make them available at no charge.

Part II: Action Step 5: Develop A Strong Marketing Campaign – How Will You Reach Your Customers And What Will You Say To Them?

The Successful Marketing Plan, 3rd Edition, Roman F. Hiebing, Jr. and Scott W. Cooper, NTC Business Books, Chicago, 2003. This is a very clear and detailed explanation of the marketing aspect of a business plan.

The 33 Ruthless Rules of Local Advertising, Michael Corbett with Dave Stilli, SummitView Publishing, Jacksonville, 2001. I have worked with Michael Corbett and Dave Stilli for more than 20 years, including writing a book with Michael Corbett. No one understands the issues of marketing a small business better. This book is indispensable for businesses that need to rely on local advertising to be successful (*www.33rules.com*).

The American Marketing Association (*www.marketingpower. com*) maintains a site with many reports, most of which are free, and useful links, all of which are related to marketing strategies.

For information about Internet marketing, including useful and free daily newsletters, you should try:

www.emarketer.com (some of its best content must be purchased)
www.imediaconnection.com
www.iab.net (Interactive Advertising Bureau)

Part II: Action Step 7: Design Your Company – How Will You Hire And Organize Your Work Force?

American Association of Franchisees and Dealers (*www.aafd.org*) has a very useful website that includes both free information and an online bookstore with publications about franchises.

Franchising 101, edited by Ann Dugan, Upstart Publishing Company, Chicago, 1998. This is an excellent collection of articles by experts on various aspects of franchising.

Part II: Action Step 9: Explain Your Financial Data – How Will You Convince Others To Invest In Your Venture?

Venture Economics annually publishes *Pratt's Guide to Venture Capital Sources*, which provides a comprehensive list of venture capital companies, along with their investment criteria and areas of focus.

The National Venture Capital Association publishes a similar directory, *National Venture Capital Association Directory*, which is also available on the web (*www.nvca.org*).

A useful site for information on bank lending, current rates and credit cards is Bank Rate.com (*www.bankrate.com*).

The Commerce Clearing House (CCH) website (*www.toolkit.cch.com*) has a great deal of useful and easy to find information including model spread-sheets, sample business plans, reports on topics of importance to small business, and legal and tax information.

Nolo (*www.nolo.com*) specializes in legal issues. Sample documents, such as contracts, are available for a fee, but most of their background material on legal issues is available at no charge.

The Edward Lowe Foundation (*www.edwardlowe.org*) is a service which promotes entrepreneurship. There is an extensive library of reports and numerous links to other business sites.

The Kauffman Foundation (*www.kauffman.org*) has a great number of resources for entrepreneurs. The reader is directed to an especially helpful site: *www.eVenturing.org.*

Accounting help, including break-even analysis, returns analysis, and creating statements, can be found in *Introduction to Management Accounting, 13th Edition*, Charles T. Horngren, Gary L. Sundem and William O. Stratton, Prentice-Hall, 2004.

Salary.com, Inc. provides a useful site for all things related to salary (*www.salary.com*).

Part III: How To Create A Time Line

Project Management: A Systems Approach to Planning, Scheduling and Controlling, 9th Edition, Harold Kerzner, John Wiley & Sons, Inc., 2005. A textbook that clearly and comprehensively covers project-management tools. For your own application, you will probably only need to refer to a few pages, so you may want to review it at a library.

The Fast Forward MBA in Project Management, 2nd Edition, Eric Verzuh, John Wiley & Sons Inc., 2005. An overview of project-management tools, and will be helpful in determining which of these tools will be appropriate to your needs.

Teach Yourself Microsoft Project 2000, Vickey L. Quinn, Hungry Minds, Inc., 2001. A good guide that will get you up and running quickly.

Part III: Present Yourself In The Best Light

How to Say It in a Job Search: Choice Words, Phrases, Sentences, for Résumés, Cover Letters, and Interviews, Robbie Miller Kaplan, Prentice Hall, 2001. A helpful guide to presenting your skills and background.

Part III: Make A Great In-Person Presentation

The Entrepreneurial Conversation: The Powerful Way to Create Mutually Beneficial, Long-Term Business Relationships, Edward G. Rogoff and Michael Corbett with Perry-Lynn Moffitt, Rowhouse Publishing, New York, 2007. Please visit: *www.thinklistenspeak.com.*

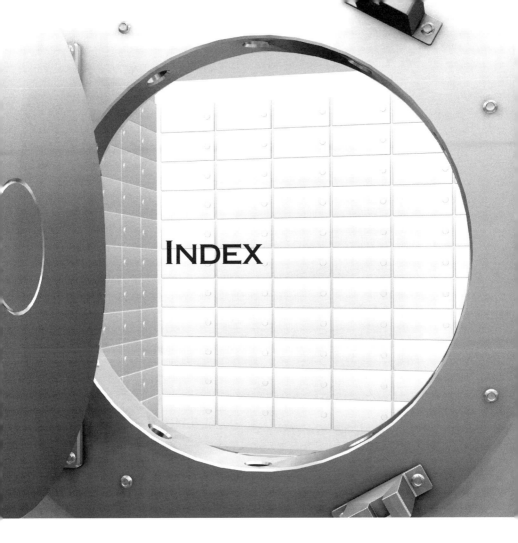

INDEX